"Lucky you, holding this book in your hands! If you're lookir
Major Arcana cards of the Tarot, you have found it! This playboc
to the cards, allowing you to discover them for yourself. Gu
joyous heart, you'll approach each card from your heart and s
meaning and intuitive guidance to read the cards with confidence and joy."

Anastasia Haysler
Painting the Soul: The Tarot Art of David Palladini

"This playbook offers creative, fun ways to get to know the Major Arcana of the Tarot. More of a
personal journal than a textbook, you'll learn by doing. In the process, you'll make these cards
your own."

Mary K. Greer
Tarot for Your Self

"I enjoyed reading this book and would highly recommend it for anyone interested in taking up
the study of the Tarot cards. I would also recommend this book for professional and experienced
Tarot readers who would like to take a fresh look at the cards."

Dinnie McLaughlin
Tarotist and Proprietor, Mystical Entertainment

"In *Mystic Spirits Tarot Playbook*, Kooch Daniels smartly offers a return to true self-exploration,
magical practice, and learning that unlocks the secrets of the 22 Major Arcana cards with modern
accessibility.

It is a gift to those who travel the path of Tarot as it offers ways to build a self-portrait of your
'magical self' while being inspired to gain access to insights from the reader's own unique experience."

Gina G. Thies
Tarot Coupling: Resources & Resolutions for Relationship
Readings and creator of *Tarot of the Moors*

"Kooch Daniels is one of the great teachers in the Tarot world. To learn from her is to learn the
powers of perception, insight, and empathy that make the Tarot come alive and its wisdom
transcendent."

Thomas Michael Caldwell
Tarot Consultant, Teacher, and Author

MYSTIC SPIRIT

TAROT PLAYBOOK

Kooch N. Daniels MA

REDFeather™
MIND | BODY | SPIRIT

4880 Lower Valley Road, Atglen, PA 19310

Other Schiffer Books by the Author:

Sacred Mysteries: The Chakra Oracle
Kooch N. Daniels, Victor Daniels,
& Pieter Weltevrede
ISBN: 978-0-7643-5711-4

Tarot at a Crossroads: The Unexpected Meeting of Tarot & Psychology
Kooch N. Daniels, MA
& Victor Daniels, PhD
ISBN: 978-0-7643-5186-0

Designed by Brenda McCallum
Type set in HP PSG/ Goudy Sans/ Alegreya

ISBN: 978-0-7643-5949-1
Printed in China

Published by RedFeather Mind, Body, Spirit
An imprint of Schiffer Publishing, Ltd.
4880 Lower Valley Road
Atglen, PA 19310
Phone: (610) 593-1777; Fax: (610) 593-2002
E-mail: Info@schifferbooks.com
Web: www.redfeathermbs.com

For our complete selection of fine books on this and related subjects, please visit our website at www.schifferbooks.com. You may also write for a free catalog.

Schiffer Publishing's titles are available at special discounts for bulk purchases for sales promotions or premiums. Special editions, including personalized covers, corporate imprints, and excerpts, can be created in large quantities for special needs. For more information, contact the publisher.

We are always looking for people to write books on new and related subjects. If you have an idea for a book, please contact us at proposals@schifferbooks.com.

Disclaimer. The material in this book is not intended to be used as treatment for any form of psychological or physical disorder. The author or publisher makes no claims or takes any responsibility for healing problems. When using the information provided in relation to the playbook, the author advises novice readers, professional card readers, and licensed practitioners of counseling and healing arts to work within the framework of their expertise.

This book is dedicated to Bailey Rose,
my crystal bright granddaughter, and all who seek
to tread the meandering, mystical path. If you're fascinated with the
Tarot and the magical realm of unknown
possibilities, these words have been written for you.

19. The Sun

CLARITY

IT'S GOOD FORTUNE TO BE YOU!
IT'S EVEN BETTER FORTUNE
TO BE YOU AND HAVE TAROT CARDS!

CONTENTS

FOREWORD

If it's a book authored by Kooch Daniels—grab it! I first became acquainted with Kooch, in the early 2000s, through her fabulous work, with hubby Victor Daniels, *Tarot d'Amour*. I invited her on my very first radio show, *Tarot Today*, and this began a long collaboration.

Kooch made more guest appearances, and I helped her create her first radio show, *Kosmic Koffee with Kooch*. She soon became a Certified Tarot Master through The Tarot Guild. I have followed her career and waited anxiously for each new publication!

Kooch now hosts her new show: *Kooch's Kosmic Kafe* on our new radio network *Psychic Talk Radio* (PsychicTalk.net). She has interviewed many of the brightest leaders in the Tarot world. Together we've invoked the sacred trumpet of Gabriel to inspire discussions about the healing powers of the Tarot and explore metaphysical resources.

A frequent figure at Ruth Ann and Wald Amberstone's Readers Studio Tarot conference in New York, she's proven herself to be a valuable teacher and positive force in our Tarot community. She has a lifetime of Tarot experience and is very knowledgeable about many forms of divination and intuitive development. Frequently, she's discussed the symbolic meanings of messages on the cards in order to find possible messages coming from the subconscious mind and has given many free mini-readings on her show.

In this book, Kooch simplifies the learning of the imagery-rich language of the Tarot, through practical and mystical guidance. The beginning Tarot student will be able to build a strong foundation in their inner landscape, and those who are experienced will find new inspiration and tools to connect even deeper with their cards.

—Dr. Dax Carlisle, DD, CTM
President of The Tarot Guild and Executive
Producer of *Psychic Talk Radio*

PREFACE

The book you now hold in your hands offers you an opportunity to take a unique Tarot journey through peaks and valleys of mystical possibilities. Its heart and soul are composed of open-ended lessons to help you develop your personal understanding of the 22 Major Arcana cards of the Tarot. Through their pictorial images, the Major Arcana cards tell stories of life and love that reflect insights of major importance to widespread human dilemmas. Some of the colorful cast of men and women represented in the cards are The Magician, The High Priestess, The Empress, The Emperor, The High Priest, The Lovers, and others who express the wizardry and wisdom of the ages.

Because there are so many books that discuss the history of the Tarot, you'll not find that information here. Instead, you're offered practical tools to help you look at the card meanings as they are reflected in your private world, which ultimately shape your interpretation of each card's meaning. Included are journaling questions that ask you to think about your life in relation to each of the major cards. Your spontaneous answers will enable you to jump into rich pools of unexpected insights to help you unveil the mysteries in the cards.

This is a playbook to enjoy, and there are no wrong answers to the questions. When you use your journal to write your outlooks, it will serve as a personal resource and recorded history of the expanding illumination of your Tarot wisdom. Although you can invite anyone to read your journal, magically speaking, its contents should be yours alone, and its sacred truths are to be shared only with those who will honor your uniquely expansive, star-studded universe. More than highlighting the steps you can take to learn the secrets in the cards, this book can increase your knowledge of the meanings of symbols, the silent language of the Tarot. When you study the pictures and images, you'll also learn to hear the subconscious voice that silently speaks to you from under the surface of your logic. You'll be connecting with the universal language of symbols that gives dreams their meanings and the ancient signs of astrology a timeless voice. More than a mystical resource, this is a book filled with opportunities to help you have a personal connection with the card images. Your personal connection with these extraordinary images will help you become an insightful card reader and develop your intuition.

The magician's axiom or truth linked to his celestial power is "Know thyself." So right now, dust off any reluctance, breathe in self-assurance, and get ready to explore your perceptions of how you experience the world. Actually, the first step is easy. All you need to do is give yourself permission to turn the page. Are you ready? Let's go!

ARTISTS AND THEIR ILLUSTRATIONS

My appreciation can't be expressed enough to thank all the
following Tarot creators who gave me permission to use their enchanting art
in my book. Each artist has their images with book location listed beneath
their name. I humbly give gratitude to the following artists
for letting me use their amazing art:

Jasmine Beckett-Griffith, illustrator, and her collaborator author
J. R. Rivera, *Beautiful Creatures Tarot*
Book beginning, The Sun:
Two-Card Spread: The Fool & The Wheel of Fortune

Steven Bright, *Spirit within Tarot*
13 Death ✦ 22 Zero The Fool

Emily Carding, *The Transparent Tarot*
10 The Wheel of Fortune; Symbols for the Four Elements/Suits

Anna Franklin, *Pagan Ways Tarot*
6 The Lovers ✦ 7 The Chariot ✦ 16 The Tower ✦ 21 The World

Kristine Gorman, *The Consigliere Tarot*
18 The Moon ✦ 19 The Sun

Dinah Roseberry and Christine "Kesara" Dennett, *A Christmas Tarot*
14 Temperance

Dinah Roseberry, *First Light Tarot*
The Star: NASA, ESA, and P. Kalas, (University of California–Berkeley, USA)
Appendix 2: Insight Cards ✦ Past (NASA, ESA, E. Sabbi)
Present (NASA, ESA, the Hubble Heritage Team [STScI/AURA],
Ack: W. Blaiar, Johns Hopkins University)
Future (NASA, ESA, the Hubble Heritage Team [STScI/AURA],
A Nota, [ESA/STScI], and the Westerlund 2 Science Team)

Robert Place, *The Tarot of the Sevenfold Mystery*
1 The Magician ✦ 20 Judgment

Beth Seilonen, *Bleu Cat Tarot*
8 Strength ✦ 8 One-Card Spread: The Emperor

Jude Simmons, *Mystic Teen Tarot*
12 The Hanged Man ✦ 15 The Devil

Gina G. Thies, *Tarot of the Moors*
Introduction: The Desert Hermit
5 The High Priest ✦ 11 Justice-Qadi

James Wanless, *The Voyager Tarot*
3 The Empress ✦ 9 The Hermit

Marie White, *Mary-El Tarot*
2 The High Priestess ✦ 4 The Emperor ✦ 10 The Wheel of Fortune

Other contributor of art:

Mikaila Beeler, artist
Owl (pg. 60) ✦ Familiar/Cat (pg. 91)

CONNECTING WITH YOUR PERSONAL TAROT MUSES

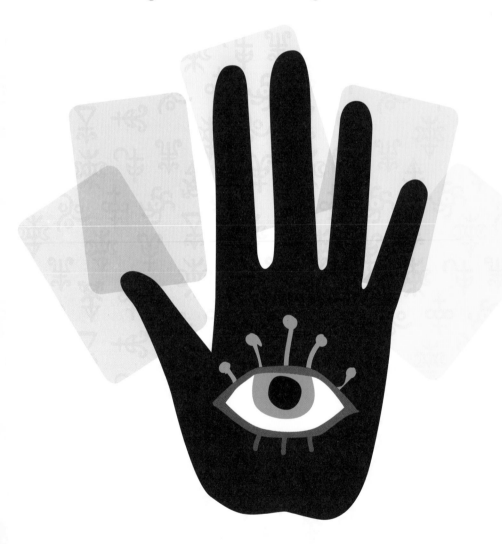

DEVELOPING YOUR RELATIONSHIP WITH TAROT SYMBOLS

IX
The Desert Hermit

Although there are various hypotheses as to the true origins of the Tarot, one aspect that everyone agrees on is that its secrets go back in time for hundreds of years. Its modern and traditional form, a deck of 78 colorful playing cards creates a picture storybook of life. In present times, these cards are most often used for personal exploration, for divination, and as a fortune-telling game to help people better understand their lives and clarify the most promising path to harmonious emotions, good health, and happiness.

An out-of-the-ordinary playing deck, the Tarot consists of 22 major cards called the Major Arcana or Major Trump. These cards symbolically portray essential, universal life qualities. Many people chose to only study the major cards, and some readers only use these 22 cards to do their readings. However, there are also 56 Minor Arcana cards. The minor cards are made up of four 14-card suits called Cups, Swords, Pentacles, and Wands. These cards can point to major life implications but, as a general rule, have less significance than the more significant 22 Major Arcana cards. In your playbook you'll mostly be developing and fine-tuning your skills to meaningfully interpret the major cards.

If you're hoping to learn how to interpret the symbols on the minor cards, you can take the information you've been given in relation to learning how to best explain the images on the major cards and apply it to becoming fearless in interpreting symbols on the minor cards. This can be done when you arrive at a comfortable destination where you accept your awareness, insights, and wisdom as the masters of relevant card interpretation. If your Tarot quest includes being given meanings for the minor cards, you're in luck as you can find numerous resources that invite you to study the minor or "lesser trump."

Many discussions you'll find here focus on your best pathway to discover the meaning of symbols. These often include techniques to **help you learn card interpretation and understand how different symbols highlight possibilities** for conversing about the cards. Here is the basic equation that points to this fundamental premise:

Symbols & Awareness of Their Meaning = Card Interpretation & Discussion

For this approach to work effectively, you must give yourself permission to view noteworthy experiences that color your ideas and give life meaning. You don't need a lengthy study of symbols to benefit from the ideas that will surface from the depths of your kaleidoscopic prisms of silent, inner knowing, but you do need to be willing to look within.

Besides offering guidance for building your Tarot skills through exploring your personal connection with symbols, you'll discover valuable divination pathways that can help build your card-reading confidence and strengthen your intuition. You'll not only learn how to interpret the messages on the major cards, but you'll be acquiring information on related practices that can help you fine-tune your awareness of a card meaning and enhance your psychic potentials. Each New Age or divinatory art that is presented at the end of each card discussion, called the "Intuitive Portal," can help you become more at ease listening to your intuition. These mystical practices can increase your Tarot repertoire and benefit your practice if you care to use them.

When you use this book to record your insights, you'll be asked to respond to questions about card images and think about how they relate to your personal world. You can record your answers to any of the questions by writing in the blank lines provided in each chapter. As you respond, if you need more space to write an answer, you might want to use an additional notebook, iPad, or whatever note-taking device you prefer.

Thousands of years ago, writing words in your own handwriting was considered a magical act. One of the main secrets hidden in a witch's black book of divination and charms was concealed in the mystery of the characters of her writing. You might not consider yourself a witch, but in modern times, your personal script, like a fingerprint, is what shows how you stand apart from others. Your personal stance becomes obvious in your written words. Of course you have choices in how you write, and even if you write your answers on these pages or just think about them. Predictably, what will become most noticeable through journaling is your progress in connecting meaningfully with the nonverbal messages in the cards. While you respond to the various questions, you'll be building a foundation of knowledge that will help you do intuitive readings (if that's what you want to do). Your contemplations will help you stand strong when you're answering someone's problematic questions that may surface while you're doing a reading. Ultimately, it's your personal insights that will reflect the guiding oracular light in each message your voice conveys when conversing in the language of the Tarot.

You'll also find astrological correspondences included with each card description. These are offered to help you expand your celestial knowledge and recognize the cosmic potency of your cards. Within the astrological discussion, you are given zodiac correspondences that will benefit your ability to probe a card's meaning through the wisdom of the Sun signs and planets. This information may come in handy when and if you find yourself discussing the card's astrological symbolism, or if you decide to include astrology as a complement to your Tarot studies.

Now, if possible, imagine awakening your inner mystic—even if you don't believe you have one. When practiced with sincerity, the questions you are asked to answer in each chapter offer a valuable pathway to help you give meaning to symbols and expand your personal connection with the major cards.

USING YOUR PLAYBOOK

When you begin using your playbook, there's one thing to keep in mind: It will benefit you the most if you're enjoying what you're doing. Adopting a lighthearted attitude, having fun, and feeling free spirited while you are using your cards and writing in your journal is one of the best ways to tap into their timeless vibrancy. If initially you don't have cards available for your practice, you can use the illustrations in this book as your resource.

You can be very logical when you are learning to use your cards, or you can invite your intuition to be part of your journey. Many readers combine logic with their intuitive analysis of their cards. Some people who are empathic or sensitive by nature often receive information through their feelings to sense a card's "message." If you are open minded and trust your "gut" or your intuition, you might find that you can retrieve information through supernormal sensing, or ESP—extrasensory perception. Some readers are clairvoyant or able to see visions through their third eye. Or, some are clairaudient and receive information through intuitive hearing. Some people are clairsentient and get information through their feelings. And some people are claircognizant and just "know" things. People who can "smell trouble" in their cards have clairsalience.

However your intuitive voice might work, when you are using the Tarot or other mystical mediums, you are choosing to walk a path that is known to increase psychic awareness and strengthen your intuitive potentials. When you say "yes" to playing with the cards, you are consciously agreeing to invoke the mysteries within them that are often hidden behind the veil of subconscious forces. What the cards offer through their imagery may provide logical references but may not have anything to do with conscious awareness. If you are fearful of using your intuition or becoming a psychic, you won't trust the information you may receive subliminally that can be used to benefit your work. If you want to do intuitive readings, the question you might ask is "Am I willing to look through my third eye?" Whatever your answer, let your studies be upbeat, and seek an engaging, positive experience.

Your first step toward learning to read the Tarot, like the first card of the Major Arcana, The Magician, is linked with invoking your passion and harnessing the power of your will. When you combine a strong desire to learn about the cards with enjoyment of practicing and playing with them, you'll be increasing your intuitive vitality and following 22 steps on the meandering path often compared with The Fool's journey.

YOUR MYSTICAL SELF

Use this following space to paste a photo of yourself. Or possibly you'd rather draw a self-portrait or sketch a creative portrait of your intuitive self. You might even add words or phrases that you cut from a magazine to create a montage about your personal "This is who I am!" Or perhaps you would like to draw the heart-and-soul reasons behind your present quest and make a coming-into-my-power collage. Importantly, this space exists for you to illustrate how you envision yourself and express your most significant feeling or passion at this present time.

....

....

....

....

Your Tarot journey begins wherever you are.

VIEWING THE WORLD THROUGH THE 22 MAJOR ARCANA CARDS

Although the Tarot is used to answer many questions concerning life's dilemmas, the main question being answered in these following pages is "How can I best learn to read the cards?" The skill-building methods you'll encounter here will guide you to explore known or unknown possibilities for interpreting symbols and card meanings. Journaling options are prompts to encourage you to free-associate ideas, fantasies, and dreams that will lend meaning to your cards. Your answers will guide you through the lens of your personal perspectives to find insights into your feelings, thoughts, observations, and intuitive reactions to understand how to best work with the cards.

Do you know the names of the 22 Major Arcana cards yet? Each of their titles holds a significant clue to finding a verbal key to unlock their secrets. For those who are just beginning to study the cards, their traditional names and numbers are the following:

Number	Title
1	The Magician
2	The High Priestess
3	The Empress
4	The Emperor
5	The High Priest
6	The Lovers
7	The Chariot
8	Strength
9	The Hermit
10	The Wheel of Fortune

11	Justice
12	The Hanged Man
13	Death
14	Temperance
15	The Devil
16	The Tower
17	The Star
18	The Moon
19	The Sun
20	Judgment
21	The World
0	The Fool

Many modern deck creators are modifying these titles. You'll notice on some of the card illustrations used inside these pages that either a new or different historical title is used. These name changes offer a way to look more deeply into the soul of the cards (and the artists) and gain additional insight into card interpretation.

Now, if you haven't already gotten out your Major Arcana cards, it's time to do so. Give a shout-out of gratitude to your Tarot muses. We're about to begin our discussion of the first major card, The Magician.

PART TWO

YOUR INSIGHTS AND THE MAJOR ARCANA CARDS

1

THE MAGICIAN

I. HERMES

Conjuring Infinite Possibilities

Playing with new ideas and an increasing sense of soul purpose ignites the desire to find fulfillment. Bold and innovative, The Magician, linked with the Greek god Hermes, stirs the cauldron of bubbling possibilities to craft an irresistible plan for success. Taking meaningful steps toward accomplishment and keeping the mind focused on the direction you want to go can turn a heartfelt dream into a realistic mission.

DIVINATORY MEANINGS

Central idea

The powerful mind

Key interpretations

Believing in the magic of your ideas, exploring potential, motivated communications, focus, initiating action, having tools to create success

Emotional associations

The first explosion of love's potency, a budding relationship, spring time of romance, sensing the potential for intimacy

Dominant mood

Confident

Astrological link

Mercury

Planetary qualities

Communication of ideas, quickness of thought, analysis, originality, Twitter, Snapchat, and networking versatility

Reversed card meaning

The need to rethink or organize your ideas

UNDERSTANDING THE MAGICIAN

Spirit Quest
Appreciation and Acceptance of Your Inner Self

As a magician or Tarot practitioner, you can only use your intuition or read the cards if you believe in your ability to do so. Let go of comparisons with others. Say goodbye to any self-doubt that you may have about reading cards. Getting in touch with the value of your ideas, no matter what they are, empowers the strength of your ability to succeed.

Magic's mystery lives in the hearts of those who believe it's possible.

Tarot Notes

✦ Which of your ideas or feelings gives you the strongest sense of being able to connect with your own inner magic?

✦ What words of advice can you give to yourself, or someone else, to increase confidence in being able to connect with the wisdom of the Tarot?

....

....

....

....

....

....

....

◆ What are your most-important Tarot dreams?

◆ What can you do on a practical level to help them come alive?

◆ In the space below, write down your dreams or goals, with the most important one at the top of your list. Don't worry. They can be changed in whatever way seems appropriate, at any time.

....

....

....

....

....

....

....

◆ Take a few moments to look at your magician card.
   What thoughts do you have about it?

◆ From your ideas, what stands out as being most meaningful when discussing your card?

◆ How are you like a magician?

....

....

....

....

....

....

....

INTUITIVE PORTAL

Manifestation

When working magic, the wand is most often used to direct energy through the power of will in order to physically manifest a desire in reality. Manifestation is the ability to speak or conjure your intentions so clearly that you feel its unfolding truth and can visualize a pathway fulfilling your goal. This is likely to happen when you mix strong desire with the confidence of positive thinking.

Your connection with The Magician's ability to manifest dreams in reality can become activated when your passion and will merge with belief in your ability to create a successful outcome. Your beliefs shape your thoughts, and with the help of your intentions, they influence your future reality. Like the Magician, use your willpower to make your life what you want it to become.

2

THE HIGH PRIESTESS

II The High Priestess

Listen with Your Heart to the Truth of Your Feelings

Your inner High Priestess hears the melody of wisdom's truth chanting in silent rhythm to the pulsating life force flowing within your being. Listening to your intuition, or ESP, enables you to feel strongly about choices that are best to make, in spite of uncertainties. Honoring your inner awareness enables you to tap into your personal power and your natural instinct for making the right decisions.

DIVINATORY MEANINGS

Central idea

Trusting your intuition

Key interpretations

Depth of insight, hearing the truth within, balancing dualities, gaining clarity, coaching or guiding others, using oracles and divination

Emotional associations

Watching waves of up-and-down emotion, sensitivity, strong feelings, opening your heart, the prospect of new relations, empathy

Dominant mood

Reflective and kind

Astrological link

The Moon

Planetary qualities

Feminine energy, emotional tides, reflection, imagination, intuition, memories, the subconscious

Reversed card meaning

Ignoring the truth of your feelings or intuition

UNDERSTANDING THE HIGH PRIESTESS

Spirit Quest
Developing Your Intuition

Can you feel "vibes" or sense what other people are going to say before they say something? In order to use your intuition, you must believe that it is possible. Trusting the wisdom of your inner self is one part of trusting your intuition. When you use the Tarot for divination or forecasting the future, you are using a time-honored resource for connecting with and developing your intuition. Many readers use their intuition to understand their best way to interpret the symbols on the cards. What Tarot reading beliefs do you have that may influence your card-reading future?

Intuition speaks silently from within.

Tarot Notes

Get into a comfortable sitting position. Take a few deep, relaxing breaths, and with your eyes closed, imagine yourself walking toward The High Priestess. With your inner, silent voice you can ask her one question. Take a moment to meditate on what question is most important for you to ask right now. Once you have a question, in your mind's eye imagine that you go to her, ask your question, and then hear her answer. What is her message to you?

....

....

....

....

....

....

Intuition or ESP is the ability to use your sixth sense and feel or penetrate truth without using words. The High Priestess uses her intuition as her pathway to wisdom. Are you able to sense your intuition working for you? If your answer is yes, what do you experience?

....
....
....
....
....
....
....
....

◆ Would you like to be a High Priestess?

◆ How would you use her powers?

◆ Do you think that a living High Priestess would worry about having a bad hair day?

....
....
....
....
....
....
....
....

INTUITIVE PORTAL

Divination

Divination is defined as calling on the divine for guidance, and seeking answers to questions by mystical means. It's the magical art of gaining insight into someone or something through sensing and/or channeling wisdom from an invisible and perhaps supernatural source. The most famous place where divination was performed was at the Delphi Oracle in ancient Greece. In present times, some people (but not all) call working with Tarot cards the art of practicing divination.

To work in a divinatory way, you must learn to develop, use, and trust your intuition, or sixth sense. Some people develop their "third eye" focus through a mystical medium such as Tarot cards. To do this, you must have the confidence that you can learn such a skill. With perseverance and persistence, by repeatedly using your cards and by asking them questions, you can be guided by your experiences to listen to your intuition and practice the ancient art of divination.

What beliefs do you have about using your intuition that may influence seeing with your third eye? In order to increase your psychic skills, you must believe that you can use them successfully. Initially, you may want to set an intention that you are going to develop your intuition. You can write your commitment in your journal or on a piece of paper or simply speak it in the moment. Be optimistic and declare that "I am trusting my intuition" or "I am developing my psychic skills." These or other similar affirmations can be valuable because your outlook influences your willingness to use your intuition.

3

THE EMPRESS

Love Is the Heartbeat of Life

The heart dares to speak, sing, and even beat in sync with alluring melodies of love. Mother Nature and her life-giving energy fertilize each moment with healing opportunities to grow and awaken to the truth of your best life direction. Making choices in accord with emotional wisdom allows you to dance freely with your passion and birth better relations with both your inner self and others.

DIVINATORY MEANINGS

Central idea
The infinite wisdom of love

Key interpretations
Nurturing/motherly energy, heart-to-heart connections, compassion,
joy, fertile possibilities, creative pathways, being in nature

Emotional associations
Romantic love, flirting, healing relations, sharing emotions,
passion, intimate or playful connections

Dominant mood
Friendly

Astrological link
Venus

Planetary qualities
Love, affection, happiness, and creative arts such as music,
singing, dance, and poetry

Reversed card meaning
Being shy or moody

UNDERSTANDING THE EMPRESS

Spirit Quest
Loving Your Unique Self

Self-love connects you with the wisdom of The Empress, who can express feelings, nurture others, and give love. It also enables you to tap into your confidence and/or ignite your passion to find resources to guide your dreams to take form.

Use the following space to draw a picture or write a song or poem that expresses your feelings and/or gives form to your creativity.

Your title: ....

The Light of Love shines within.

Tarot Notes

Romantic notions can shape reality and expand or contract present and future choices. When you think about the power of love, what feelings do you experience? What words do you hear in your mind when your internal voice describes love?

....

....

....

....

....

....

....

✦ What are three memories or feelings you associate with love?
   However you answer this question, is it possible to discuss your thoughts from the unconditionally loving view of The Empress?

✦ How do or don't you express your voice of love?

....

....

....

....

....

....

....

+ How does The Empress speak to you?

+ If you were to have a conversation with her, what might you discuss together?

+ Think about the qualities you have that can be compared with those of The Empress. What are they?

Reread the key words listed above that are associated with the planet Venus and this card. What idea in the "Planetary qualities," is most important in relation to your view of Venus and The Empress?

....

....

....

....

....

....

....

....

....

....

....

....

....

....

....

....

....

INTUITIVE PORTAL

Positive Affirmations

Positive affirmations are words you say to yourself either out loud or silently in an upbeat, encouraging, respectful way. These words or phrases are often messages to yourself to affirm that you're doing a good job, or doing your best, or that you can have successful experiences in life and love. You can repeat them numerous times like a chant or chorus of a song. For an affirmation to have benefit, it's best to say it from a positive point of view.

The following are some examples of positive affirmations:

"I am loving and have good communications with myself and others!"

"I am capable of doing good work and winning!"

"I will be a successful Tarot card reader!"

"I am confident of my ability to find meaning in Tarot images!"

"I am developing my sixth sense and using my intuition!"

4

THE EMPEROR

IV The Emperor

Your Thoughts Build the Foundation for Your Future

Willful, logical, and naturally competitive, The Emperor asserts his power with a firm grip. Wearing the crown of leadership, he courageously acts to help generate prosperity. Right or wrong, his ideas are most often spoken with a sense of bold confidence. Emotional control and psychological command reveal his strength and authority. He is the companion to The Empress, and his internal heat ignites the surging union of positive and negative energy.

DIVINATORY MEANINGS

Central idea
Acting with strong will

Key interpretations
Being confident, assertive or forceful ideas, controlling behavior,
the competitive spirit, pondering moneymaking potentials
or strategies for success

Emotional associations
Being logical, influencing, or dominating in relation to commitments,
making choices concerning romance, turning on fiery charm

Dominant mood
Bold

Astrological link
Aries

Sun sign qualities
Fiery will, pioneering spirit, the warrior, assertiveness,
courageous, adventurous

Reversed card meaning
Arrogance

UNDERSTANDING THE EMPEROR

Spirit Quest
Achieving Your Goals

To achieve success, it's important to know what goal you want to reach. When you have a goal in mind, step by step, you can move with the tides of worldly ebb and flow toward fulfillment. Similar to The Emperor, who is steadfast in asserting his will, focusing on your plans and being confident provides incentive to knock on the door of opportunity.

Your power to succeed lies within.

Tarot Notes

✦ How strong is the force of your willpower?

✦ How do your feelings about your ability to take the lead affect your present choices?

....

....

....

....

....

....

....

- ✦ Find the space within your body where confidence lives.
  What does it feel like?
- ✦ What are your beliefs that link with your sense of confidence?
- ✦ How might the words you used to answer these questions help or hinder
  your ability to walk your Tarot path?

....
....
....
....
....
....
....

- ✦ Do you know any people who have emperor qualities?
- ✦ How do you relate to this type of person?
- ✦ If you were an emperor in charge of great treasures, would you invite
  others to share your secret stash of riches?

....
....
....
....
....
....
....

CARD INTERPRETATION SKILL

Title Analysis

Analyzing the *name* on a card offers an excellent means to understand the *meaning* of a card. Look at any Major Arcana card title and think about what it means to you in your day-to-day world. You can be practical or philosophic in order to find clues that point to its potential meaning(s).

Right now let's analyze the title of the card called The Emperor. What is the dictionary meaning for the word "emperor"? Besides powerful man and ruler, do you know of any other synonyms for the word? What does being an emperor mean to you? How do actors who play the movie role of an emperor act? How might your answers to any of these questions give clues about how to interpret The Emperor card?

5

THE HIGH PRIEST

The Heart of Good Feelings

The High Priest, a.k.a. The Hierophant and The Teacher, walks a sacred path where inner awakening has value equal to a precious diamond. Besides having affiliations with Western spiritual traditions, he may be initiated into secret orders that include training in healing arts such as Tantra, alchemy, hypnotherapy, and relationship mediation. When actively fulfilling his responsibilities, he can prove through his actions that he deserves a seat among those reputed to be wise.

DIVINATORY MEANINGS

Central idea
Connecting with a higher purpose

Key interpretations
Listening to inner wisdom; being real; seeking soul truth; finding a mentor, teacher, shaman, or spiritual guidance; integrity

Emotional associations
Dancing to your heart's song, finding answers to romantic concerns, loyalty to love, bonding with friends, commitment

Dominant mood
Straight forward

Astrological link
Taurus, The Bull

Sun sign qualities
Determination, being down to earth, practical efforts, being rooted to your truth, loyalty

Reversed card meaning
Confusion

UNDERSTANDING THE HIGH PRIEST

Spirit Quest
Feeling Gratitude

Even during tough or uncertain, complex moments, you can count your blessings and focus on your enduring strength of spirit. Having a sense of gratitude creates a forward momentum that supports finding a purposeful path and realizing your highest potentials.

Your present choices shape your future.

Tarot Notes

The High Priest has gratitude for all things, large and small. He stubbornly listens to the truth of his inner wisdom and doesn't rely on the truth of others. Can you hear and follow your heartfelt truths when they are silently unveiled? What do you know about yourself that triggers your sense of gratitude?

....

....

....

....

....

....

....

....

....

Look at your card The High Priest. What is your unique point of view regarding his role? Use your imagination to think about what questions he might like to ask you. Use the following space to discuss your thoughts.

....

....

....

....

....

....

....

....

Perhaps you have encountered a High Priest in a movie, in a book, or in a classroom. How would you describe him to your best friend? Now imagine that you are playing a real-life role of The High Priest, and a longtime friend asks you about romance. She wants to know if she has found true love with her new boyfriend. From your High Priest perspective, how might you answer her question?

....

....

....

....

....

....

....

....

....

....

INTUITIVE PORTAL

Meditation

Find a quiet space, breathe deeply, and relax your body and mind as much as you can. Close your eyes and silently listen to or witness your thoughts. There is nothing else to do right now except look within. Clear your mind of restless thoughts as much as possible, and let your thoughts move toward inner reflection and a nonjudgmental state.

Now consciously breathe slowly and more deeply. Take a few moments with your eyes closed to contemplate the image called The High Priest. What do you sense about him? From your reflective, meditative state, ask your inner self to think about the role The High Priest might play to benefit your immediate intuitive development. What do you imagine that he might ask of you, or what commitments might he suggest that you make at this present time?

6

THE LOVERS

VI

The Lovers

The Magic of Love Can Happen Anywhere at Any Time

Reaching out to others and embracing the pleasure and sometimes pain of intimate communications can be like a lush garden abundant with fragrant blossoms of heartfelt awareness. Emotional relations can inspire bonds of commitment that reveal the brilliance of the soul's light. The receptive lovers can easily climb the highest mountains to find pleasure's delight, but if dark clouds overshadow their sincerity, they can misstep and fall from love's path.

DIVINATORY MEANINGS

Central idea
Inspirational and uplifting emotional wisdom

Key interpretations
Abundant joy, love, mutual respect,
making the right choices, overcoming doubt or fear to
open your heart, heartfelt sensitivity

Emotional associations
Romance, heart-to-heart communication, partnership,
courtship, intentional flirting, sharing affection, experiencing
magic in the moment

Dominant mood
Happy

Astrological link
Gemini, The Twins

Sun sign qualities
Versatility, high-spirited thinking, inquiring or curious, penetrating
perception, mental and physical vitality, dualistic thinking

Reversed card meaning
Vulnerability or jealousy

UNDERSTANDING THE LOVERS

Spirit Quest
Gaining Insight into the Color Tones of Emotions

People often associate colors with different behavior, emotions, and moods. For example: You might hear about someone who is so angry that he or she is "seeing red." Or you might know someone who had to buy a red car because it feels so "hot" to drive. Or someone else might tell you that she is sad and "feeling blue" or "green with envy." Another person might wish they had more "green" in their pocket.

Often, Tarot readers interpret the feeling tone and meaning of a card by using their own associations with its colors. You might find that sometimes your associations to the colors on a card can trigger your intuitive sense about its meaning. Look at your cards and take a little time to think about all their different colors and the feelings you have in relation to them.

Love is not always logical.

Tarot Notes

If you were to paint a picture of yourself being in love, what colors would you use? Do you see any of these same colors in your Lover's card?

....

....

....

....

....

....

Is there any color that is predominant in your Tarot deck? If your answer is yes, what does this color tell you about it? What is your favorite color in your deck?

....

....

....

....

....

....

....

....

Love is a wonderful feeling, but sometimes, loving feelings can change or sour.

✦ How do you and your friends discuss or react to negative emotions such as jealousy or a love relationship breaking apart?

✦ When looking at The Lovers card, how might you interpret its image in relation to insecurity, lack of trust, or other complex emotions?

....

....

....

....

....

....

....

....

CARD INTERPRETATION SKILL

Observing Dominant Colors

Below is a list of colors, many that you might see on your cards. On the line next to the name of each color, make a note of one or more key words that you associate with it. Don't overthink your answers. Write your responses quickly in relation to how a color pops out at you and grabs your attention. For example, if you are searching for meanings connected with the color red, your answer might read something like this:

Red: The color of Valentines, intense emotions, anger, and the flow of blood

Use the lines below to create your own list of associations that you have with each of the following colors:

Red: ....
....

Green: ....
....

Purple: ....
....

Blue: ....
....

Yellow: ....
....

Orange: ....
....

White: ....
....

Black: ....
....

7

THE CHARIOT

Steer Your Sense of Purpose with Intention

The Chariot's wheels turn in the direction of adventure, progress, and victory. When you are rushing toward your goals, willpower, focus, and determination are needed to keep a steady course of action and overcome ambivalence or indecisions. As your earthly momentum becomes more impassioned, you'll have a stronger sense of what choices have the highest potential for fulfilling your dreams.

DIVINATORY MEANINGS

Central idea
Evolution

Key interpretations
Progress, being pulled in two opposite directions at one time, seeking
an intuitive path, focusing on adventures, reaching for your goals

Emotional associations
Seeking clarification about love's direction,
balancing emotional perspectives or contrary feelings, traveling
for romance, a heated kiss

Dominant mood
Ambivalence

Astrological link
Cancer, the crab

Sun sign qualities
Depth of feeling, the ebb and flow of emotions, the mother,
domesticity, loyalty to love, using your intuition

Reversed card meaning
Indecision

UNDERSTANDING THE CHARIOT

Spirit Quest
Learning about Symbols

Symbols speak a nonverbal language that uses images, marks, or signs to represent something. As you begin to understand the meanings of Tarot symbols, you're also learning to understand the messages being shared without using words. For example, when you see an arrow, most likely you'll look where it points. Or, if you're looking at an emoji with a smiling face that has hearts in place of eyes, most likely you'll view it as a positive message. You don't need to see written words to understand what it's telling you as it silently speaks through its image.

Many symbols are recognized throughout history and different cultures to have the same or nearly the same meaning. A smiling face symbolizes happy emotion if you see it on a Renaissance painting in the Louvre (the most famous museum in France), or if you see it on a modern-day Tarot card.

Another example is the chariot's wheel. It can represent the revolving momentum to move forward on the path of life, or your power to stay on course. In the space provided below, draw a circle or a wheel. You might want to add decorations to it. At the bottom of your symbolic drawing, give it a meaningful title.

Your title: ....

Use the wisdom of both your head and your heart.

Tarot Notes

◆ How is a chariot like a car?

◆ If you could go anywhere in a chariot, where would you want to go?

◆ When you are traveling a highway and you get to a crossroad, do you trust your intuition to help you decide which way to go?

....

....

....

....

....

....

....

◆ Can you imagine yourself driving a chariot?

◆ What does it look like?

◆ What do you think that you might see when you're sitting in the driver's seat?

◆ How do you envision yourself arriving at your destination after a five-hour ride in your chariot?

....

....

....

....

....

....

....

- Have you ever watched a movie in which people used chariots as their vehicles?

- If your answer is yes, what did you learn by watching people drive them?

- How might your answer influence your interpretation of The Chariot card?

....

....

....

....

....

....

....

....

....

....

....

CARD INTERPRETATION SKILL
Understanding Symbols

Look at the images on your major Tarot cards or view the pictures of the cards in this book. When you look at each major card, pay attention to the symbols. As you're viewing each card, notice which symbols visually stand out the most. Most likely, these are the ones most important to you.

Although there are many different ways to discuss and interpret card symbols, you have the freedom to free-associate your own ideas about their potential meaning. The meanings you give to each symbol will influence your interpretation of a card. The following statements are examples of giving interpretations to symbols:

Symbol: An old person
Interpretation: Dealing with old emotional issues or seeking a mature perspective

Symbol: Someone wearing a red cape
Interpretation: The inability to hide anger or passion

Symbol: A skull
Interpretation: Something is dead or changing in an unpredictable way

Symbol: The reins used to drive a chariot
Interpretation: The power to direct or control active forces

The following is a short list of some universal symbols that you might see in your cards. Although there may be multiple meanings given to each symbol, here you are mostly given only one meaning:

SYMBOL	A POTENTIAL MEANING
Altar	A sacred space
Ankh	Eternal life
Arrow	A penetrating force
Bird	The ability to soar above concerns
Blossom	Opening to the new
Bones	Underlying structure
Butterfly	Transformation
Cat	Familiars, magical spirit or potential
Chalice	Vessel to hold emotions, the element Water
Coins	Finances, material concerns
Crown	Success or leadership
Dogs	Animal nature, loyalty
Dove	Peace
Feather	Inspiration, power to soar
Fire	Quick action or reaction
Fish	Money

Flowers	Budding opportunities
Grains	Fertility
Hand	The ability to reach
Horses	Travel
King	Ruler, control
Key	Unlocking something of import
Letter	A message
Lion	Strength, endurance
Mother	Domestic or nurturing authority
Owl	The ability to see in the dark or use your intuition
Pentacle	Material concerns, the element Earth
Rabbit	Fertile possibilities
Rose	Purity
Stars	Light, clarity, hope
Snake	Secrets or hidden feelings
Sword	Sharp ideas, the element Air
Trees	Knowledge, growth
Wands	Creativity, the element Fire
Water	Emotions, flowing energy
Waves	Up-and-down emotions
Wheel	Progress

Look at the following list with names of the 22 major cards. Next to each title make a note of the key symbol from each card that is most important to you. Then in a few words, describe your personal associations with each symbol.

1 The Magician ....

2 The High Priestess ....

3 The Empress ....

4 The Emperor ....

5 The High Priest ....

6 The Lovers ....

7 The Chariot ....

8 Strength ....

9 The Hermit ....

10 The Wheel of Fortune ....

11 Justice ....

12 The Hanged Man ....

13 Death ....

14 Temperance ....

15 The Devil ....

16 The Tower ....

17 The Star ....

18 The Moon ....

19 The Sun ....

20 Judgment ....

21 The World ....

0 The Fool ....

STRENGTH

(This is Major Arcana card 11 in some decks.)

Strength Is a Winning Force

Whether strength implies physical power and forcefulness or humility and a gentle touch, its vigor arises from the silent bravery of the inner spirit. Determination, willpower, fortitude, focus, and the daring heart influence the magnitude of its mighty expression. If you call yourself a soldier or lover, worldly or spiritual minded, self-confidence and personal mastery will come into focus when your inner strength is reflected in the mirror of self-knowledge.

DIVINATORY MEANINGS

Central idea
Potency and power

Key interpretations
Having physical strength, feeling courage,
seeing positive results, meeting the inner hero, boldly stepping
toward a challenging event

Emotional associations
Magnetic attraction, instigating romantic opportunities,
saying "yes" to love, having positive responses
to challenging communications, lust

Dominant mood
Courageous

Astrological link
Leo, the lion

Sun sign qualities
Passion, creativity, optimism, enjoyment of the limelight,
playful and fun loving, romantic

Reversed card meaning
Lack of strength or too much ego

UNDERSTANDING STRENGTH

Spirit Quest
Taking Time to Play

Your strength is more apparent when you connect with your inner core and let your mind rest from life's stress and pressures. Taking time to "recharge your battery" can also help you connect with your personal power. Playful time enables you to balance the yin and yang of your vitality, launch your plans with ease, and pursue your interests with enthusiasm.

Your strength is radiant like the sun.

Tarot Notes

Take this moment to envision your own personal courage.

✦ What words and thoughts empower your sense of strength?

✦ If you were the maiden on the Strength card, how might you describe your inner and outer forcefulness?

....

....

....

....

....

....

....

....

Find your center of strength. From this perspective, consider if you want to give readings to others or only use the cards for reading for yourself and personal discovery.

✦ What beliefs are affecting your decision?

✦ If you're already giving readings, are you able to be objective when you read for yourself?

✦ Can you read successfully for yourself?

....

....

....

....

....

....

Close your eyes and visualize a superstrong person lying in the sunshine on the beautiful beach. Now, imagine feeling this person's physical strength existing within you.

✦ Can you imagine feeling this type of strength in a difficult situation that you have recently encountered?

✦ From an empowered point view, how might you react to your past challenging encounter?

....

....

....

....

....

....

INTUITIVE PORTAL

Animal Communication

"Meow-meow-meow, read my purrrrfect mind," said the cat climbing high in a tree.

Do you have a cat, dog, or other pet? If you have close contact with any animal, do you ever sense what it is thinking? Some readers will use their cards to try to communicate with their pets or answer questions concerning them. At other times, people will visit a Tarot reader to ask questions about their pets. Let's imagine that someone is reaching out to you for a reading to answer the question "Will my pet be found?" Even if you don't consider yourself to be pet psychic, or animal communicator, you can pull one card to ignite thoughts about their lost furry friend.

To do a one-card reading to answer such a question, simply fan and place your 22 Major cards facedown on your table. Next, ask your question. Without looking at the front of the cards, select one.

If you aren't familiar with a card's meaning, you can look at the key interpretations for the card that you've selected. Do any of these words or phrases give you a sense about finding the lost pet or not? What does your intuition tell you?

For a demonstration one-card reading, let's imagine that you selected The Emperor card. In the "Key interpretations" section listed for this card, it states the importance of "being confidant" and "pondering strategies for success." Even though The Emperor card doesn't say "yes" or "no" specifically, it gives positive encouragement in the form of the instruction to look for strategies that will help you find the pet and stay confident. With this interpretive insight, instead of worrying about losing a pet, I might discuss taking actions that could help find the lost pet, such as circulating lost-and-found notices or calling the humane society. If you don't have any sense of an answer to your question from the one card you select, you can pull another to help you gather greater insight. You can also consider reforming the question, or attempt to read the pet.

A one-card reading to gather insight

9

THE HERMIT

IX

Hermit

Solving the Mysteries of Your Life

The Hermit or Wise One, who can be either feminine or masculine, walks a path of self-reliance carved from a rock-hard foundation of honesty and integrity. Self-knowledge acquired through inner effort awakens the certainty of knowing the best choices you can make to solve the riddles of life. Often holding a lantern with a light equated to the mystical Star of David, this sojourner has the wisdom to clarify and search for timeless truth and inner freedom.

DIVINATORY MEANINGS

Central idea
Listening to inner wisdom

Key interpretations
Independence, self-reliance, freedom from unnecessary worries,
soul searching, self-effort and discipline, truthful communications,
financial know-how

Emotional associations
Selfless love; keeping one's cool,
even during relationship uncertainties; balanced emotions;
clear heart-to-heart communications

Dominant mood
Adaptable

Astrological link
Virgo, the virgin

Sun sign qualities
Powerful ideas, down-to-earth communications, hard working,
shoulders responsibility, good with money, success minded

Reversed card meaning
Uncertainty or under too much pressure

UNDERSTANDING THE HERMIT

Spirit Quest
Trusting "Gut Instincts"

Sometimes we hear other people's ideas, and we want to agree with them. *Yes, yes, I want to believe what you say and do what you ask*, you think. But even before you can speak such words, you feel a knot in your stomach. Can you imagine what your stomach is trying to communicate when you feel such a knot? What happens if you ignore an intense gut instinct?

Physical sensations in your body are its way of asking you to listen to your truth spoken from within. They are nonverbal, sensory messages from within your body that give blatant clues to your internal reactions. Oftentimes an instant knot in the stomach is a warning that you aren't comfortable, and that you need to be cautious when approaching a situation or take time to think about what you want to do in relation to it. If you feel an adrenalin rush of energy in your body, it's a sensory message that is asking you to be on high alert to what is going on within and without your being.

Many times, people have a first impression or "sense" about someone, or a gut response to meeting a person. It might not be logical, but it is exclaiming a subconscious truth. Imagine this example: An attractive person draws your attention, and you'd love to get to know him or her better. Unfortunately, your gut instinct is warning you through knots in your stomach that something isn't right. Your immediate question might be this: Do I give into my desire to talk with this person, or do I pay attention to my internal warning system and politely walk away?

When you listen to your gut response, you still need to pay attention to common sense. If you have an intense desire to date a married person, it may feel like you're having a positive gut response in response to this person. At the same time, your common sense may be sending out a red warning signal. When your common sense disagrees with your gut response, you need to weigh the merits of both voices; you need to listen to your inner dialogue and analyze what response is in your best interest. Most likely you've heard someone say, "If I would have only listened to my intuition, I would have saved myself a big problem." For many, the opportunities to learn to trust the murmurings of their intuition come through multiple trial-and-error experiences.

Ignoring your instinct equals ignoring your treasure chest of wisdom.

Tarot Notes

Sometimes we listen to other people's ideas and ignore our own. Successful intuitive outcomes rely on following one's own truth. The Hermit, or "Way-Shower," who is mentally strong, has attained the ability to look within the reflective pool of the subconscious mind. He stands alone holding his lantern, illuminating light of wisdom so that he can help others see their higher path more clearly.

Use the following space to write a poem or draw a picture of The Hermit's lantern and its soul-warming light:

Your title: ....

Philosophically, The Hermit's ability to shine the light on one's path has great value. If you place your Tarot cards next to a magical lantern that illuminates truth, how do you think others might respond to your cards?

....

....

....

....

....

....

....

....

When you have time, close your eyes, breathe deeply, and look into your third eye. From this inner perspective, ask your intuitive self to give you a new insight into the role of The Hermit. What do you sense or see from your third-eye vision about his message?

....

....

....

....

....

....

....

....

CARD INTERPRETATION SKILL

Dialoguing with Images

You can develop more awareness of the meaning of each major card by looking at its central figure and having a make-believe dialogue with it. Let yourself imagine that you can use your intuitive sense to understand the thoughts of the prominent individual or figure on every card. Then picture yourself having a conversation with this character about their most important role and what message he, she, or it might have for you. What part of your discussion is most significant to you?

For an example, let's look at The Hermit: What visible qualities about his manner of being in the world are most prominent? If he could talk, what might he tell you? Perhaps he would ask you to shine a positive light on your secrets, or delve into your love life. Or, maybe he would want you to think about a practical course of action that could lead you to success.

In this moment, what question would you like to ask The Hermit (or any other of your favorite images)? Now close your eyes and imagine that you see The Hermit, and then ask your question. What answer do you receive? Do you have any "gut feelings" in response to his answer? Don't worry if you get more than one answer or if your answer to the same question changes over time.

10

THE WHEEL OF FORTUNE

X The Wheel of Fortune

Endings Often Lead to New Beginnings

The Wheel of Fortune spins, bringing change to thrust us forward around the game board of life. Its whirling motion can carry us to the top of our aspirations, where our ambitions are fulfilled, or reversely it can descend, pushing us into a lowly pit of exasperation. Good fortune gathers momentum when we keep our faith and continue to search for a way to quench our thirst for happiness in spite of the unpredictability of our fate.

DIVINATORY MEANINGS

Central idea

Fortune and fate

Key interpretations

Good destiny, prosperity, potential change, positive perspectives,
moving up and down along busy highways of life

Emotional associations

Playful teasing, changing perspectives, expanding awareness about
love's potential, enjoying romantic moments, affection

Dominant mood

Trusting

Astrological link

Jupiter

Planetary qualities

Kindness, ambition, philosophy, motivation, generosity,
seeing the bigger picture, higher education

Reversed card meaning

Uncertain change

UNDERSTANDING
THE WHEEL OF FORTUNE

Spirit Quest
Seeking Good Fortune

Many people have routines, rituals, or superstitions that they follow, with the hope that it will make it easier to get where they want to go and find ways to win over obstacles. Some keep lucky coins or crystals in their pockets, others frame the first dollar that they made when starting their business, others throw salt over their left shoulder, and some silently call their spirit guides. What approach, either from outside voices or those within your mind, do you follow to improve your chances for finding good fortune?

....

....

....

....

....

....

....

Play to win the Game of Life.

Tarot Notes

Imagine that The Wheel of Fortune has the potential to move you forward toward success. What goals are you hoping to reach?

....

....

....

....

....

....

....

In your mind's eye, visualize yourself sitting in front of an ancient sorceress named Fortuna, who is strangely beautiful and is known to grant good fortune. You can ask her any question in relation to your personal quest. After you think of a good question, silently ask her for its answer. After she stirs her ancient cauldron with a broken spoon, she offers you a star-shaped crystal, a blue cat's-eye bead for good luck, and a Chinese fortune cookie. Imagine taking the cookie and breaking it open to see a note. Looking from within your third eye, what message do you see?

....

....

....

....

....

....

....

- ✦ If you were offered a prize on the spinning Wheel of Fortune, what would you like to win?

- ✦ Are you willing to set an intention and make a commitment to seek your winner's fortune?

Use the lines below to describe what you want to win and what you will do with your success.

....

....

....

....

....

....

....

....

....

....

CARD INTERPRETATION SKILL

Recognizing the Four Elements
Air, Water, Earth, and Fire

The four elements are the comprehensive, symbolic foundation of the 78 cards of Tarot. They give thematic clues to help unveil primary meanings within the cards.

Each element occurs specifically as one of the four Minor Arcana suits, which consist of 14 cards. These four suits symbolically point to the rhythmic dance of life in relation to mind (Air), emotions (Water), body (Pentacles), and spirit (Fire). The characteristics of each of the four elements point to ways you can discuss the cards in the Minor Arcana suits.

The imagery connected with the different elements is also scattered throughout the major cards. For instance, The Wheel of Fortune is often illustrated with an image of one of the four elements sitting in each corner of the card. These are represented by the four fixed signs of the zodiac: the bull (Earth–Coins), linked with Taurus; the lion (Fire–Wands), for Leo; the eagle (Water–Cups), sign of Scorpio; and a human (Air–Swords), representing Aquarius.

Air: The Mind
Tarot Suit of Swords or Crystals

> Corresponds to the power of ideas, mental understanding, keen awareness, lofty visions, analysis, and the Sun signs Gemini, Libra, and Aquarius

Water: Emotions
Tarot Suit of Cups or Chalices

> Corresponds to emotions, underlying feelings, intuition, gut instincts, imagination, flowing energy, and the Sun signs Cancer, Scorpio, and Pisces

Earth: The Body
Tarot Suit of Pentacles or Coins

> Corresponds to the body, being grounded, money / the financial world, motivation, career efforts, and the Sun signs Taurus, Virgo, and Capricorn

Fire: Spirit
Tarot Suit of Wands or Rods

> Corresponds to creativity, passion, willpower, enterprise, inspiration, desire, active energy, and the sign signs Aries, Leo, and Sagittarius

JUSTICE

(This is Major Arcana card 8 in some decks.)

Inner Truth Equals Outer Balance

Nothing escapes the all-seeing eye of Truth as the Scales of Justice, depicted as Qadi (a judge), objectively weigh, measure, and mediate the merits of mind, heart, and spirit. Even if deception lies hidden far beneath the surface, at some crucial point truth rises like a phoenix in emotive transparency. The shifting winds of change move with the ebb and flow of karmic tides to balance uncertain issues with perfect precision.

DIVINATORY MEANINGS

Central idea
Weighing and balancing pros and cons, rights and wrongs

Key interpretations
Equality, finding your Chi or center of balance,
developing self-control, mediating opposites,
searching for harmony, diplomacy

Emotional associations
Balancing sensitive emotions, positive vs. negative moods,
making romantic choices, meaningful relations, learning to trust

Dominate mood
Passionate

Astrological link
Libra, the balance

Sun sign qualities
Balance, harmony, concerns for others, artistic expression,
improving relations through fair negotiations

Reversed card meaning
Imbalance

UNDERSTANDING JUSTICE

Spirit Quest
Checking Your Attitude

Our attitudes and outlooks, and keeping our mind receptive to new ideas or, conversely, keeping our mind closed to new ideas, influence our day-by-day realities. Think about how different attitudes can affect the way you feel. For example, you might have an optimistic attitude about playing sports or feel joy in relation to a joining a team. How would such a perspective make you feel about playing sports compared to feeling pessimistic or doubtful about your athletic ability?

Comparatively, your attitude about your intuition also influences how it will work for you. The different ways you think about it influence how it plays out in your daily life. Keeping your conscious mind open to strengthening your intuition and believing in your sixth sense can benefit a positive inner dialogue that can nurture your psychic development.

Be optimistic about your intuitive ability.

Tarot Notes

Close your eyes and look inwardly with your mind's eye for the center point within your physical body. Can you find your body's center of balance? Where is it? If you sit in one position and move your torso back and forth, it can help you locate this physical place of balance within your body.

....

....

....

....

....

....

◆ Imagine using the Scales of Balance to weigh your dominant feelings, and find the truth that matters to you in this moment.

◆ Are you balancing any pros versus cons? If your answer is yes, what do you imagine could happen if you place your feelings on a Scale of Balance?

....

....

....

....

....

....

....

◆ What do you do either physically, emotionally, or mentally to honor your intuition?

◆ How might this practice best serve you if you're talking about the Tarot to another person who is skeptical of balancing their mental and intuitive energies?

....

....

....

....

....

....

....

INTUITIVE PORTAL

Using the Pendulum

A pendulum is a bead, crystal, button, or stone that hangs like a weight from the end of a short string or chain. Some readers work with a pendulum alongside their Tarot cards to clarify answers to yes-or-no questions. They are often used to answer questions such as "Does he love me?" Or "Will I be happy if I change jobs?"

When you have a pendulum, hold the top of its cord in your right hand, between your thumb and index finger. Silently ask a yes-or-no question. Then let its weight fall freely above your pulse point on the wrist of your left hand. (Your left hand is closest to the wisdom of the heart.) It should hang above your wrist but not touch your skin. The stone will respond to the heat in your body's pulse and start to gently swing.

Silently observe its movement, and watch what direction it goes. If the stone or bead moves up and down in the direction from your wrist to your elbow, the answer to your question is yes. If its movement is horizontal across the width of your wrist, the answer is no. If it swings in a circle, the answer is maybe, or it's letting you know that an answer is not yet available.

THE HANGED MAN

12 *The Hanged Man* ♆

Freedom Is a Gift You Give Yourself

The Hanged Man feels secure within himself on his suspended quest to find a safe haven to dive into unknown depths of inner possibilities. Practicing austerities, he yearns to be his own person, to follow the path of self-discipline, and to resist the dictates of convention. Hanging upside down in self-sacrifice, he longs to listen to his intuitive mind and hear timeless truths that transcend the merits of logic. Faith and trust is his bridge to cross the tumultuous River of Life as he adventures to find the healing balms of awakening.

DIVINATORY MEANINGS

Central idea

Unexpected insight into truth

Key interpretations

Extraordinary ideas, gaining new perspective,
unusual circumstance, unexpected turn of events,
inner guidance, seeking a spiritual path

Emotional associations

Contemplating romance, emotional sensitivity,
dreaminess, inundating waves of feelings, experiencing
passion's depth, love for God

Dominant mood

Anti-authority

Astrological link

Neptune

Planetary qualities

Watery depths of emotions, intuition, dreaminess, fantasy,
illusion and delusion, spirituality

Reversed card meaning

Feeling misunderstood or separate from others

UNDERSTANDING THE HANGED MAN

Spirit Quest
Feeling Vibrations

When you believe that your intuition can work for you, you open the door to using your third eye. If you believe that you have six senses, instead of five, you gain an additional sense to help guide your awareness. Right now I'm asking you to keep your mind open and believe that you feel the energy in images and intuit the meaning in Tarot symbols.

Take out The Hanged Man from your stack of major cards. Once you have your card, put it face up and hold your open palm about an inch above its central image. Then close your eyes. Now, let your intuition *feel* the image. Connect with its energy. What do you *feel* or i*ntuitively hear*? What unknown story does your card silently sing to the heart of your intuitive self?

When you're playing with your cards, listen to your intuition.

Tarot Notes

Being true to yourself means walking a path aligned with your truth, even if it's different than what others expect. What thoughts or unique outlooks, like The Hanged Man dangling upside down from the Tree of Knowledge, inspire you to "walk to the beat of a different drummer"?

....

....

....

....

....

....

- ✦ Realistically, do you have any ideas that make you feel "hung-up"?
- ✦ Can you put a positive spin on these thoughts?
- ✦ If you were The Hanged Man looking upside down at life, how might it look?

....
....
....
....
....
....
....

- ✦ Do you feel a "soul calling" to read the cards?
- ✦ Does The Hanged Man point to a way to connect to your sense of developing your intuition in any way?

....
....
....
....
....
....
....
....

INTUITIVE PORTAL

An Intuition Game

This game works best when you believe that you can intuitively communicate and feel Tarot images. Take three major cards of your choice out of your deck and look at their faces. For demonstration purposes, let's imagine that you are selecting The Magician, The High Priestess, and The Hanged Man cards. You may want to put your palm over each card's central image and ask your intuition to sense their symbolic energies.

After looking at the front of the cards, turn them facedown, shuffle them, and then place them facedown in a horizontal line on a flat surface. You should now have three facedown cards sitting randomly in a horizontal row in front of you.

Now close your eyes and use your internal vision to find The Hanged Man. You may want to put your open hand over your cards to experience the feeling of each card. When you feel ready, select and turn over the card of your choice that you're sensing will be The Hanged Man.

If you find him with your first intuitive guess, great! If you didn't, try again to find him by intuitively selecting another card from the remaining two facedown cards.

After you have found The Hanged Man, play this same game again. Practice is one key to strengthening your intuitive ability. When this game becomes too easy, play it with five facedown cards in your horizontal row instead of three.

There is only one rule when playing this game: Have fun!

DEATH

A Caterpillar Has to Die to Become a Butterfly

You may unpredictably experience an emotional detour that inspires a dismaying twist and unsettling shift in how you view reality. Keeping your mind open to unexplored possibilities allows you to perceive a sudden change as the undeveloped soil of renewal. When you reach a dead end and confront the impact of not being able to move ahead as intended, search for an agreeable solution that shines a light on improving your current situation.

DIVINATORY MEANINGS

Central idea

The birth of new possibilities

Key interpretations

Changing circumstance or perspective,
new beginnings, revival, unknown outcomes,
viewing an expanded horizon, transformation

Emotional associations

Anticipating romantic change, death/rebirth of emotional
understanding, intense communications about feelings,
hidden truth, intimacy

Dominant mood

Anxious

Astrological link

Scorpio, the scorpion

Sun sign qualities

Strong emotions and attachments, willful, secretive,
powerful intuition, partnership minded, tolerant unless angry

Reversed card meaning

Uncertainty

UNDERSTANDING DEATH

Spirit Quest
Creating Positive Transformations

Imagine that you can turn fanciful ideas into powerful opportunities to design a revitalizing renaissance. What intentional changes in yourself or in society would you like to make that can inspire positive change? Your ideas don't have to be grand or cost a lot of money. Even small steps taken over time can lead you toward a meaningful rebirth in your relations, your career, or even your Tarot practice.

Hope for tomorrow brings promise for a new day.

Tarot Notes

Some people are afraid of the Death card. Are you? What do you think might be the differences between an optimistic interpretation of the Death card and a negative one? Hint: Instead of loss, the Death card can indicate rebirth and progress.

....

....

....

....

....

....

....

- Why do you think skulls are drawn to adorn jewelry, shoes, purses, and clothing?

- Do you ever wear anything that is decorated with a skeleton or skull? If yes, what do you feel when you wear it? If no, what do you feel when you see other people wearing something decorated with a skull or symbol of death?

....

....

....

....

....

....

....

- Through times of rebirth, change, or expected or unexpected endings, what thoughts enable you to feel more safe and secure?

- What do you experience as the most-visible opportunities for change or transition for you at this present time?

....

....

....

....

....

....

....

....

INTUITIVE PORTAL

Using Magical Charms or Protective Amulets

Whenever doing any kind of Tarot or divinatory work, many readers, sages, sorcerers, and sorceresses call upon mystical traditions to protect subtle (invisible) energies. Sometimes people wear crystals, magical charms, or protective amulets as part of a necklace, bracelet, or ring. Because amulets can appear to be a piece of jewelry, who would ever suspect that magical intentions such as opening the third eye or blocking unwanted energy are included with their fashion statement?

Also, some readers use healing crystals, seashells, charms, amulets, or talismans to remove or reduce fears and bring different levels of interpretations to their card reading. A person getting a reading might be asked to pull a magic charm from the trinkets kept inside a secretive pouch. The chosen trinket will add symbolic significance that will impact the card's interpretation. For example, someone getting a reading selects the Death card. The reader then decides to ask this person, who is acting dismayed, to also pull a charm from his or her magical pouch to add insight into how best to interpret the Death card. If the selected charm is a silver car, the reader might then include a discussion about unexpected treks or changes in travel plans. Perhaps the suggestion that the client possess protection in the form of a picture of Christ or a spiritual teacher inside his or her car will decrease any sense of dread concerning unknown future changes. Or, if a heart charm would be selected to accompany one's interpretation of the death card, a reader may discuss the importance of keeping the mind open to new romantic possibilities, or holding on to faith and trust during any transformative or enigmatic emotional process.

14

TEMPERANCE

Balancing between the Earth and the Sky

The angelic spirit of Temperance balances opposites in the wave-free pool of moderation. Not being too hot or cold, not acting weak, but yet not too bold, keeps the elixir of life flowing evenly between solar-masculine and lunar-feminine forces. With one foot grounded in practical thinking and the other foot diving into watery subconscious depths, the heart and mind can meet in the middle to explore a spiraling equilibrium of present possibilities and future potentials.

DIVINATORY MEANINGS

Central idea

Walking the middle path

Key interpretations

Moderation, reflecting on inner truth,
connecting with your angels or protective forces,
learning to say "no," harmonizing opposites

Emotional associations

Balancing heartfelt concerns, balancing yin
(negative energy) with yang (positive forces), setting boundaries,
attraction of opposites

Dominant mood

Feeling centered

Astrological link

Sagittarius, the archer

Sun sign qualities

Expansive or philosophical thinking, higher education, ambition,
idealism, generosity, love of travel

Reversed card meaning

Ignoring inner wisdom

UNDERSTANDING TEMPERANCE

Spirit Quest
Performing Acts of Random Kindness

A random act of kindness is performing an act that has the potential to affect someone in a beneficial way without letting the person know about the good deed that you have done. Putting money in a stranger's parking meter so that he or she doesn't get a ticket is an example of a random act of kindness.

Spreading happiness is a simple way to create unexpected miracles in the world. You can selflessly and secretly do something, either big or small, to help another person. Most acts of random kindness have a positive affect on the world. Often, our own happiness happens naturally when we focus on making others happy.

Jeannine Carson created a fun Tarot experience called Random Acts of Tarot. She suggests randomly leaving a Tarot card for a stranger to find. This arbitrary act can inspire the stirring of the cauldron of our collective consciousness. On her website, the Tarot Coach, she claims that:

"It makes us pause for a moment, in the middle of the hustle and bustle of modern life, and think about ourselves, the image, and possibly even about the person who left it. Why did I notice this card? What does it mean to me? What is the story in the imagery?"

The Tarot world is a better place because you're in it.

Tarot Notes

What does temperance mean to you? One of the four cardinal virtues, it embraces living in moderation. When you have a moment, use your favorite resource to look up the word "temperance." What do you find out about it that is relevant to your life and taking a Tarot pathway?

....
....
....
....
....
....
....

Sometimes when deciding what action to take, we are facing decisions that could take us in opposite directions. For example, you might have to decide between two opposing desires, such as saving money for the future or going on a spending spree today. Or perhaps you want to say "no" to going to a dance club, but your best friend is encouraging you to say "yes." When you have to make a choice, do you bring your intuition into your decision-making process?

....
....
....
....
....
....
....

For a moment, use your imagination and pretend that you are a majestic rainbow filling the sky. How do you feel balancing the energies of the rain and sun? In the space provided below, draw a rainbow or any other symbol that you connect with balancing opposites (or write a poem or song).

INTUITIVE PORTAL

Communicating with Angels

Some people believe in angels. Do you? Some readers use angel card oracles to channel angel messages in the same way a Tarot reader can use intuition to meaningfully interpret symbols. Cards such as Temperance that have images of angels can point toward the potential of conversing with these celestial beings.

Angels, associated with divine light, are able to help people overcome spooks of ghostly fear. They are believed to do good deeds like healing the sick and bringing what is most needed at the exact time of need. The names of celebrated angels of the major cards include Michael (card 14), Gabriel (card 20), and Raphael (card 6).

For those who believe in angels, there is a mystical art of communicating with them that most often involves meditation, prayer, and the unconditional belief that it is possible. To connect with angels, you can verbally invite them into your life. Before going to sleep, innocently ask for their love, assistance, and protection. You might light a candle or incense or offer a flower before silently giving voice to your message.

THE DEVIL

15   *Devil*   ♏

Optimism Overrides Negative Thinking

You may unpredictably experience an emotional detour that inspires a dismaying twist and unsettling shift in how you view reality. Keeping your mind open to unexplored possibilities allows you to perceive a sudden change as the undeveloped soil of renewal. When you reach a dead end and confront the impact of not being able to move ahead as intended, search for an agreeable solution that shines a light on improving your current situation.

DIVINATORY MEANINGS

Central idea
Negative forces

Key interpretations
Confronting the shadow, internal struggle or external challenges, overindulgence, frustration, malice, manipulation or intimidation

Emotional associations
Doubts or insecurities about love, miscommunication or confusion, feeling guilt or betrayal, jealousy, holding on to fear, facing loss

Dominant mood
Conflicted

Astrological link
Capricorn, the mountain goat

Sun sign qualities
Determination, reliability, financial intelligence, being practical, grounded, and sure-footed in the world.

Reversed card meaning
The need to use caution or protect oneself

UNDERSTANDING THE DEVIL

Spirit Quest
Embracing a Positive Attitude

Remove the letter *d* from the word "devil," and what is left is the word "evil." Linked with fear, guilt, addiction, sin, and Lucifer, the fallen angel, it's easy to obsess about a wide range of negative attributes connected with this image.

When devilish energy gets tough, remember that you still have a reserve of feel-good possibilities that can change a frown to a smile. Developing inner courage to transform pain into gain, or problems into opportunities, is a form of personal power that improves one's chances for avoiding potholes of negative energy.

Wear an invisible cloak of loving energy.

Tarot Notes

What are your beliefs about the devil? Are they related to religious beliefs? In the space provided, briefly explain how you would describe the devil to a five-year-old child. Would this explanation be any or all of your description of The Devil card if you were explaining it to an adult?

....

....

....

....

....

....

....

People can say or do things that are hurtful or appear to be negative, but you don't have to respond to their negativity or become fearful. Sometimes, however, fear is an appropriate response as this reaction tells you clearly that you need to protect yourself. Do you fear the devil?

....

....

....

....

....

....

What do you think or feel when you see The Devil while playing with your cards? Readers can sometimes interpret this card with a pessimistic voice. How devilish of The Devil card to inspire negative thinking! When looking at this image, take care. Even if it makes you look at insecurities (and it may not), find ways to view challenges as opportunities and difficult situations as pathways for learning.

When you are selecting cards and laying them on your table, the card that sits to the left of The Devil card communicates the type of influence this card may embody. For instance, if The Empress was randomly selected to sit next to The Devil, I might interpret this card combination as a serious temptation in love's playground. Or, if by chance The Hanged Man would be selected to sit next to The Devil, I might reflect on how I'm hung up in situations where I'm feeling stuck in negative thinking.

The following spaces are for your thoughts about The Devil card.

....

....

....

....

....

....

INTUITIVE PORTAL

Learning Psychic Self-Defense

Many people who teach New Age Tarot skills offer the White-Light Meditation to create a beneficial shield of psychic protection and guard against negative energy. Through this contemplation, you create an invisible defense shield from fear or other draining energy.

Although people may think it important to take classes in martial arts and learn how to protect the outer body, sometimes they may forget to protect their internal being. It's especially important to feel safe and protected when working with cards, practicing the art of divination, or going ghost busting. If you feel afraid or vulnerable when shuffling Tarot cards, it is a strong warning to not do this type of work. Perhaps at some later time, you'll feel confident when working with them, and then it's time to resume your shuffle.

When you hold on to positive thoughts, they are like a bright light that repels darkness. One way to fortify positive thinking is to envision your inner being as an expanding spark of the flame of divine love. This following meditation helps you cultivate faith in your ability to protect your energy and stay calm during stressful times:

The White-Light Meditation

First, do your best to quiet your mind. Then close your eyes and imagine a brilliant flame glowing near your heart. Either with thoughtful words or your imagination, direct this light to burn brighter and grow larger. Next, imagine that this light expands to reach all the way from above the top of your head to beneath the bottom of your feet and that you are completely surrounded by a protecting shield of vibrant, white light. Endeavor to feel its healing warmth and silently affirm, "*I am protected by Divine Light and Love!*"

16

THE TOWER

The Tower

At Times, a Fall Is Unavoidable

Sometimes our towering ambitions can ascend far beyond the solid foundation of practical reality. When decisions, made with the hope of fostering success, seem to go wrong, we may feel like we've been hit with a thunderbolt. Keeping calm when our looming expectations crumble, and exerting the courage to rebuild what has shattered beyond our control, enables us to effectively rise like the phoenix from the ashes and constructively direct our efforts.

DIVINATORY MEANINGS

Central idea
Something takes a tumble

Key interpretations
Stress, negative or toxic circumstance,
obstacles on one's path, falling from grace, power struggles,
being bullied or intimidated

Emotional associations
Feeling vulnerable, misunderstood, stifled,
or hurt; loss of loyalty; broken trust or ties of affection;
upsetting communications

Dominant mood
Grumpy or antisocial

Astrological link
Mars

Planetary qualities
Competitiveness, assertiveness, boldness,
fast and fiery actions, anger

Reversed card meaning
Needing to fix what is broken

UNDERSTANDING THE TOWER

Spirit Quest
Letting Go

Sometimes we make mistakes, but we are not our mistakes. When we make mistakes or feel self-doubt, it pushes us to learn what is important in the big picture of who we are becoming. If we measure our self as being too tall or too small, too wide or too narrow, our eyes forget to see how much beauty lives deep inside. If a tower (either literal or symbolic) starts to fall, let go of holding on, get out of harms way, find safe and secure ground, and focus your will on what helps you flourish.

Breathe in trust, and breathe out love.

Tarot Notes

When expectations crash, our sense of self-worth and security can come tumbling down. Have you ever fallen from the tower of noble ideals or principles? If your answer to this question is yes, what did you learn from your experience?

....

....

....

....

....

....

....

- ✦ What inner qualities enable you to repair crumbling towers of circumstance?
- ✦ How might these qualities become part of your interpretation of The Tower card?

....

....

....

....

....

....

....

....

- ✦ When your inner being is completely shaken, how does your attitude affect the way you feel?
- ✦ What advice might you give to a friend whose life is undergoing an experience that you can compare with being hit by a thunderbolt?

....

....

....

....

....

....

....

....

INTUITIVE PORTAL

Aromatherapy

Sometimes when a client sees a card with a falling tower, his or her response might be "Oh no!" Depending on the interpretation a reader gives to this card, a person can walk away from the reading feeling hopeful or hopeless. If a person shows anxiety in relation to The Tower (or Death or The Devil), a reader can reframe doubts or fears into strategies for personal growth. Talking about positive possibilities combined with the healing properties of herbs can be an upbeat means to counterbalance worries about complex emotions or negative circumstance.

Some types of aromatherapy can be perfect partners to accompany Tarot readings. If a client is going through difficult times, scented herbs can stimulate well-being. Even readers can use herbal remedies to feel good. One practice that many readers use to improve their own or their client's sense of well-being is smudging. With good intentions, a reader will light either sage or sweetgrass, like incense, and let the smoke purify the air in their reading space. Along with cleaning the air, it can also clear and relax the mind. If you plan to use aromatherapy during a reading, first ask if your client is allergic to any herbal scents. The following short list of common herbs is said to inspire positive qualities:

Spice or Herb	Beneficial Properties
Garlic	Protection, banishes negativity
Lavender	Relaxation, promotes happiness
Mint	Clarity, to invoke prosperity
Rose	Love, purifying energy
Rosemary	Emotional strength
Sage	Protection, purifying energy
Thyme	Vitality, high energy
Cinnamon	Health, successful communications

You may be asking what aromatherapy has to do with developing your intuition. One benefit of using aromatherapy is that it can help you relax. The more relaxed you are, the more receptive you are to listening to your intuitive voice.

17

THE STAR

Shining Your Light in the World

Throughout history, the stars have been viewed as a predicable map of knowledge that can help people navigate across uncharted seas of earthly adventure. Children are taught to "wish upon a star" as their twinkling light brings hope to see "truth" beyond the darkness and confusion. Radiant, their celestial energy inspires the trust that the "sky's the limit" and that it may be possible to discover realities that are unknown and go beyond the limits of physical boundaries.

DIVINATORY MEANINGS

Central idea
Gaining insight

Key interpretations
Clarity, hope, optimism, letting go of limiting beliefs,
reaching out to network, focusing on priorities, star gazing with a
winning attitude, the healing force of celestial inspiration

Emotional associations
Illumination of love's potential, an outpouring of happiness,
reaching for fulfillment in romance, dancing with passion,
trust in commitment

Dominant mood
Lighthearted

Astrological link
Aquarius, the water bearer

Sun sign qualities
Mental vitality, confidence, independence, rebellious ideas,
unselfishness, heartfelt concern for humanity

Reversed card meaning
Seeking clarity

UNDERSTANDING THE STAR

Spirit Quest
Viewing the Constellations

When possible, take some time to gaze upon the stars twinkling in the nighttime sky. Can you recognize the Big Dipper or any of the zodiac constellations? Have you ever sighted the planets Mercury, Mars, or Venus? Learning about the constellations connects you with the energy and vastness of starry space and hints at the enormity of cosmic consciousness.

Stargazing illuminates cosmic pathways.

Tarot Notes

How might a starry bright attitude change how you feel about your most dominant current concerns? If you could "wish upon a star," what wishes might you make?

....

....

....

....

....

....

....

In the space below, draw a picture of a star. Even if you make a simple line drawing, sketch a symbol illustrating your hopes, wishes, or intentions for your future in the center of the star. When you combine the star with your symbols in its center, what does your image represent?

....

....

....

....

....

....

....

Your title: ....

+ What inspires you to reach for the stars?

+ Do you have a role model or mentor who inspires you to connect with the highest sense of who you are and who you're becoming?

....

....

....

....

....

....

....

INTUITIVE PORTAL

Scrying and Crystal Ball Gazing

Scrying is looking into a crystal ball, or a shiny object such as a mirror, and seeking a vision that may give an answer to a question being asked. It's not uncommon to see a crystal ball sitting on a reader's table next to her Tarot cards. She may use it for its magical properties, to create an ambiance, or for scrying.

Most often a reader will gaze into her ball hoping for a message with value or a glimpse at an image that offers insight into a pertinent story. If you want to try this, first ask a question and communicate it either out loud or silently to your crystal ball. Then look deeply within your globe and ask your intuition to "see" what's important. Be patient while you're looking.

When you look into your ball, tuck logical thinking into your pocket and let intuition be your guide. Some people say that to see into a crystal ball, mirror, or other shiny object, you need to be clairvoyant (a psychic or visionary who sees mental pictures). What's most important is having faith in your ability to "see" something and being open minded to receiving a message, however it may come.

If you believe that you can't see anything in your scrying surface, change or reframe your present belief to "I'm learning to dive psychically into my crystal ball and intuit messages from its depth!" Turn on your mind's right channel and experiment with the belief that you can see stories unfolding within it. You have to disconnect from logical looking. It can also help if you focus into but beyond the center of your ball and slow your impatience and expectations. Ask to be shown an answer to a question or receive a message from an ancestor. Yes . . . you CAN do this!

18

THE MOON

THE MOON-XVIII

Entering the Doorway to the Subconscious

Celebrated for its changing phases, the Moon reflects sunlight and brightens nighttime darkness. Its luminosity influences the feminine cycle, and its magnetic currents penetrate watery depths and keep ocean waves in ebb-and-flow motion. Because lunar energy is believed to stimulate the subconscious mind, The Moon card relates to our underlying emotions and the memory, imagination, intuition, and fluctuating sensitivities.

DIVINATORY MEANINGS

Central idea
Depth of emotion

Key interpretation
Dancing in moonlight, nourishing your imagination,
trusting intuition, deep reflection, motherly love, surfing waves of
memories, esoteric experiences

Emotional associations
Experiencing the power of love, emotional surges,
strong mental currents effecting underlying feelings, sensitivity,
domestic or romantic affections

Dominant mood
Dreamy

Astrological link
Pisces, the fish

Sun sign qualities
Nurturing, compassion, emotional sensitivity, creativity,
imagination, and naturally intuitive

Reversed card meaning
Feeling overly emotional

UNDERSTANDING THE MOON

Spirit Quest
Developing Emotional Patience

Learning to be patient is an advanced mystical skill. This inner capacity enables a person to be calm when things don't seem to be going as planned. If time isn't moving fast enough to keep you content, or when emotional currents in the River of Life become stagnant from the chaos of wrong actions or choices, patience can help you find inward balance. Being centered enables you to make better choices and focus on the right opportunities. Importantly, it can also help you hear the murmuring voice of underlying emotions and have access to your intuition.

Your third eye exists to help you see better.

Tarot Notes

✦ What are your strongest emotions in this present moment?

✦ How do you express them?

✦ Can you sense their truth if you feel impatient?

....

....

....

....

....

....

Intuition, also called the sensitivity of sixth sense, ESP, seeing with your third eye, and the psychic sense, is often linked with lunar energy.

✦ Do you feel a connection between the Moon and its influence on your intuition?

✦ Would you like to do an affirmation to enhance your intuitive reflections? If so, please repeat the following statement: "I trust my intuition and use it well."

....

....

....

....

....

....

....

....

When possible, go outside at night and view the full Moon. What do you feel when you see the moon in the sky, and how does this compare with what you feel when you see The Moon card?

....

....

....

....

....

....

....

INTUITIVE PORTAL

Working with the Phases of the Moon

You can watch the movement of the Moon as it journeys through the sky, and chart its energetic changes on a lunar calendar. Throughout time, people have planted their gardens in relation to the lunar cycle and observed how our emotional nature is affected by its phases. Because of its effect on the psyche, the position of the moon, or its phases, can have a direct influence on your intuition and your Tarot readings. With awareness you can experience how The Moon's energy in its different phases affects you.

Waxing Moon
> The Moon's light increases as it grows full

> *Phases of the waxing Moon*
> **New Moon**: new beginnings, time to plant seeds of new ideas
> **First Quarter Moon**: increases energy
> **The Full Moon**: maximum lunar light and reflective awareness

Waning Moon
> The Moon's light decreases

> *Phases of the waning moon*
> **Third Lunar Phase**: assessing ideas
> **Last Quarter Moon**: low tides of lunar and worldly energy
> **Dark of The Moon**: absence of lunar light

19

THE SUN

THE SUN XIX

When the Sun Is Setting in the West, It's Rising in the East

As the dawning of each new day bursts forth, the ascending Sun passionately shares its exuberant light and warmth. Equal to the Sun's brilliant qualities, this card is linked with inspiration, personal growth, creativity, sprouting the seeds of life, and connecting with the radiant force of healing. Its glowing light allows ideas to grow in the fertile ground of earthly achievement and success.

DIVINATORY MEANINGS

Central idea
Personal growth and creative self-expression

Key interpretations
Creativity, having a sunny disposition, courage to reach for the top,
prosperous thinking, confidence, enthusiasm,
warmth of friendship

Emotional associations
Being optimistic about love, feeling charmed by romance, receiving
gifts from another, healing the heart of past mistakes

Dominant mood
Cheerful

Astrological link
The Sun

Planetary qualities
The life force, positive solar energy, precision, logic, masculine
wisdom, being inwardly awake, inspiration, creativity, growth

Reversed card meaning
Uncertainty or self-doubt

UNDERSTANDING THE SUN

Spirit Quest
Choosing Happiness

Is happiness a choice? Some people claim that sitting in the Sun makes them happy. Think about what you do that inspires feelings of joy. Also, think of past things you have done that put an expansive smile on your face.

Take a moment and make a list of different things you enjoy doing that make you happy. Whenever you feel restless or anxious, take out this list and ask yourself to do one of these activities.

....

....

....

....

....

....

Enjoy fun in the sun, smile big, and take a selfie!

Tarot Notes

✦ Do you notice any differences when you play with your Tarot cards in the warmth of the Sun compared to when you use them at night?

✦ Do you notice any differences in how you view your cards when you play with them when you're feeling warmhearted compared to when you're feeling stress?

....

....

....

....

....

....

Do you have an intuitive sense about the meaning of the Sun card? If so, how might the image on your Sun card and what you feel about it mirror your own present feelings?

....

....

....

....

....

....

Imagine that you are talking about the meaning of this card with a friend who is having romantic problems. What might you say to him or her about The Sun in relation to a challenging love crisis and bruised feelings? Would your discussion of this card change when you're talking about happy emotional concerns?

....

....

....

....

....

....

CARD INTERPRETATION SKILL

Becoming Familiar with Zodiac Card Correspondences

Astrology has many different aspects. The most basic form of astrology is the brief daily or weekly forecasts that you can find online or in newspapers. Even though these weekly zodiac forecasts may not be in depth, you can read them for fun and to learn a little astrology. Your Sun sign can be found on the following list of the twelve Sun signs and their calendar dates. This list also contains the title of the Major Arcana card that corresponds to each Sun sign or planet. For example, in Western astrology, if you are born on March 28, you will read on the chart that you're an Aries, and the card associated with your Sun sign is The Emperor.

Most Tarot cards, especially the ones with images that follow historical traditions, have astrological correlations. Because zodiacal symbolism relates to specific qualities, it is a time-honored reference used for card interpretation. Although it's an optional study, many people who read the cards use astrology to expand their oracular insight. In this playbook, the correspondences between the Tarot and the zodiac are quoted from a divinatory system first used by an occult society existing in the late 1800s and early 1900s, known as the Hermetic Order of Golden Dawn. The BOTA (a religious organization dedicated to spiritual attunement) and Arthur Waite, co-creator of the Rider-Waite deck, have popularized it. You can find other astrological correspondences linked to the cards.

One person who made a change in the Golden Dawn's system was Aleister Crowley, creator of **The Thoth** deck. He modified it to correspond to his vision of the New Age. If you're already using astrological correspondences from a different system than the one listed here, don't be alarmed. It's best to continue using the one you have already adopted as long as it's working well for you. Make sure that you listen to what your intuition tells you about a card's astrological imagery, and let it contribute to your overall sense of what the zodiac can add to your interpretative insight.

Sun Signs and Major Arcana
Connections

Dates	The Sun Signs	Corresponding Major Arcana
March 21–April 20	Aries	The Emperor
April 21–May 20	Taurus	The High Priest
May 21–June 20	Gemini	The Lovers
June 21–July 20	Cancer	The Chariot
July 21–Aug 20	Leo	Strength
Aug 21–Sept 20	Virgo	The Hermit
Sept 21–Oct 20	Libra	Justice
Oct 21–Nov 20	Scorpio	Death
Nov 21–Dec 20	Sagittarius	Temperance
Dec 21–Jan 20	Capricorn	The Devil
Jan 21–Feb 20	Aquarius	The Star
Feb 21–March 20	Pisces	The Moon

Planets and Corresponding
Major Arcana Cards

Planets	Major Arcana Correspondents
Sun	The Sun
Moon	The High Priestess
Mercury	The Magician
Venus	The Empress
Jupiter	Wheel of Fortune
Mars	The Emperor
Saturn	The World
Neptune	The Hanged Man
Pluto	Judgment
Uranus	The Fool

JUDGMENT

Tranquility Balances the Judging Mind

Looking through the lens of a superior attitude or the critical mind can result in judgment of others. We can also be a kind or cruel judge viewing our own self or wondering about angel Gabriel's judgment of our psyche. In a transformational sense, judgment can be the voice that commands us to stay even minded, especially if someone is putting us down for choices deemed inferior, or if we feel that we are being judged unfairly.

DIVINATORY MEANINGS

Central idea

Awakening to a new reality

Key interpretations

Dealing with criticism, changing circumstance,
voicing opinions, arousing judgments, dramatic decisions,
rite of passage, renewed faith, karma

Emotional associations

Love's transformations, surrendering to change,
judging emotions, communication breakthroughs or breakups,
waiting for a call or kiss

Dominant mood

Secrecy

Astrological link

Pluto

Planetary qualities

Psychic awareness, strong impulses, stolen love,
long-distance relations, unpredicted change or rebirth,
soul transformation

Reversed card meaning

Fear of change

UNDERSTANDING JUDGMENT

Spirit Quest
Assigning Qualities to the Meaning of Numbers

Do you like some numbers more than others? What's your favorite number? Do you have beliefs or superstitions about it? If so, what are they?

Take some time to think about your associations with numbers. What are your observations about them?

Use the following list of numbers 1 through 9 and the blank space that follows them to discuss and fill in any feelings, ideas, or beliefs that you have concerning them.

For example, let's look at the number 1: It's the number of beginnings, starting projects, taking the first step. I connect it with the elephant-headed god, Ganesh, the Hindu deity, because when you are starting something, or taking a first step toward a goal, he is believed to help when he is asked. His mantra: Aum Gang Ganapataye Namah.

Number   **Your Feelings and Ideas about Numeric Qualities**

Number 1: ....

....

Number 2: ....

....

Number 3: ....

....

Number 4: ....

....

Number 5: ....

....

Number 6: ....

....

Number 7: ....

....

Number 8: ....

....

Number 9: ....

....

Numbers are symbols that you can count on!

Tarot Notes

Take a moment and use your intuition to feel the image on the Judgment card and consider what it personally means to you. Next, think about its potential meanings in relation to your logic and emotions. What do you discover?

....

....

....

....

....

....

....

....

◆ In your past, have you ever been judged unfairly?

◆ How did your physical body feel when being judged by another?

◆ Are you willing to "forget and forgive" those who were critical minded or made "snap judgments" about you?

◆ Does another person's comments about someone affect your own feelings about the same person?

....

....

....

....

....

....

....

◆ If you think you're intuitive, is this your truth or your judgment?

◆ If you were explaining your answer to the angel Gabriel, how do you think he might respond?

....

....

....

....

....

....

....

CARD INTERPRETATION SKILL

Exploring Mystical Meanings of Numbers

Before the birth of Tarot, numerology was used to search for insights into cosmic patterns and possibilities. Ancient seers would use their intuition to understand the tone and meaning of the potential of a number's vibration and link them with human characteristics such as mental sharpness, emotional temperament, and intellectual or intuitive abilities.

Each of the 9 single-digit numbers is esoterically assigned meanings linked with different forces or universal personality traits. Here is a partial list of some of their key qualities and behaviors:

Number	Qualities
Number 1:	Dynamic energy, the first step, birthing possibilities
Number 2:	Emotions, intuition, imagination
Number 3:	Expansion, ambition, creativity
Number 4:	Organizing, hard working, thinking outside the box
Number 5:	Communication, overthinking, money minded
Number 6:	Love, beauty, balance
Number 7:	Sensitivity, intuition, dreamy yet purposeful
Number 8:	Responsibility, focus on values, assertiveness
Number 9:	Wisdom, clarity, empowerment

When doing numerology, every multiple number must be reduced to a single digit between 1 and 9. For example, the number 10 becomes a number 1 by adding its numbers together:

$$10$$
$$1 + 0 = 1$$

Or the number 11 equals 2 when you add its numbers together:

$$| |$$
$$| + | = 2$$

Numerology and Major Arcana Cards

Every card in the Major Arcana has a number. Some diviners use numerology to interpret a card's deeper meaning and expand their insight by drawing connections between cards that share the same number. To illustrate how to do numerology in conjunction with the cards, let's look at the Judgment card and its number, 20. We add together the numbers in 20 by adding 2 plus 0, which equals 2. By doing numerology, the numeric tone of the Judgment card equals 2.

$$20$$
$$2 + 0 = 2$$

Two other major cards also have this numeric vibration: Justice and The High Priestess. Because The High Priestess is card number 2, we don't turn this number into a single digit, since it's already one. The other Major Arcana card with a number that equals 2 is Justice, card 11. We find this card's number when we add 1 + 1 and find that its sum equals 2. The universal number 2 is linked with strong emotions, intuition, and imagination. To add your intuitive awareness when interpreting these three cards that each have the number 2 numeric vibration, look above and review what you have written about 2 in the section "Spirit Quest: Assigning Qualities to the Meaning of Numbers." Read your own description of your personal connections with the number 2. What you have written about this number will add awareness and depth to your interpretation of all three cards that share this numeric vibration. Let's imagine that I use the terms "polarity," "duality," and "partnership" and USE MY INTUITION for my personal connections for number 2. For each card that has the 2 numeric vibration, some or all of these words will be part of my interpretation when I discuss their meaning.

For all major cards past The Hermit, numbered 9, you must do simple numerology to find a card's single digit. To push open the door to viewing the kinship between major cards and numerology, the following chart gives the numeric vibration for all major cards.

Number	Numeric Energy of the Major Arcana Cards
Number 1:	The Magician, The Wheel of Fortune, and The Sun
Number 2:	The High Priestess, Justice, and Judgment
Number 3:	Empress, The Hanged Man, and The World
Number 4:	The Emperor and Death
Number 5:	The High Priest and Temperance
Number 6:	The Lovers and The Devil
Number 7:	The Chariot and The Tower
Number 8:	Strength and The Star
Number 9:	The Hermit and The Moon

The connections between Tarot and numerology are vast. If you're interested in learning more about this art, there are many valuable resources that you can easily find.

THE WORLD

Fill Your World with Splendor

After personal exploration, journaling, and Tarot discovery, you have reached the final major card, The World, threshold to accomplishment. It can represent an awakening of worldly maturity that arises from an increased sense of who you are and who you're becoming. Here, unexpected gifts of knowledge gained from experience can set us free to rise out of the ashes of yesterday's mistakes to ignite today's wisdom and bring greater possibilities for tomorrow's victory.

DIVINATORY MEANINGS

Central idea

Opportunities for resolution, wholeness, or completion

Key interpretations

Victory, achievement of goals, arriving at the finish line,
successful problem solving, being in the right place
at the right time, travel

Emotional associations

A kiss awakens commitment, heartfelt affection,
a renewed sense of love; relation resolution;
a sense of wholeness; finding your truth

Dominant mood

Empowered

Astrological link

Saturn

Planetary qualities

Maturity, responsibilities, passing of time, structure, organization
skills, connecting with deep values

Reversed card meaning

Frustration

UNDERSTANDING THE WORLD

Spirit Quest
Creating a Sacred Space

After doing readings or having a psychic or intuitive experience, we often need to recharge our mind, emotions, and spirit. And sometimes, if we have experienced a stressful situation, we may want to take time out from our busy life to reflect on our feelings or the results of our choices.

When the outside world is too hectic or full of demands, creating an inner sanctuary is a beneficial contemplation for healing our body and spirit. To do this, first close your eyes and let your mind move into a meditative space. Inwardly think about, design, feel your magic to create, and visualize an inner space filled with objects that are sacred to you. Perhaps your imagination will design a room with a vaulted ceiling, oriental rugs, and 22 lit candles, or maybe you'd like to envision yourself being outdoors in nature, sitting within a circle of trees next to a makeshift altar decorated with your favorite Tarot cards, amulets, deities, and crystals. You have limitless choices to decide what you want to include in your sacred space.

Once it's created, let your mind feel the peace, healing energy, and beauty of your inner sanctuary. You can revisit your sacred space at any time. But when you linger there, let your internal dialogues focus on connecting with your inner healer or intuitive muses, who can guide you to feeling the best that you can feel.

Ask your intuition to help you solve the riddles in your life.

Tarot Notes

The world is rich with opportunities for you to find what you need. Balancing your voice of reason with the truth in your heart will help you navigate the meandering pathways to find your way.

In relation to how you see yourself in the world, complete the following two phrases:

....

"I want" ....

....

"I need .... to be happy."

Supercharge your potentials by believing in your ability to succeed. Because the world is filled with polar opposites such as positive and negative, attraction and avoidance, and passion and dispassion, patience and perseverance are usually needed to arrive at your desired destination. Every time you say "yes" or "no" to daily circumstance, your direction becomes more defined.

What you believe and how you feel lays the foundation for your willingness to step forward into the world of Tarot. Think about the following statements and answer if they're true or false for you. Although they may appear odd at this point in your reading, your answers indicate your readiness to divine with the cards.

True or false:

———— I am an optimist!

———— I can do what I want to do.

———— I am an intuitive!

———— I depend on others to tell me the meanings of symbols.

———— I love my Tarot cards.

Whether you use your Tarot cards solely for your own use, or if you are doing or hoping to do readings for others, your confidence will help you be receptive to hearing their silent messages. What words of advice can you give yourself to help you tap into greater card-reading confidence?

....

....

....

....

....

....

....

CARD INTERPRETATION SKILL

Connecting Key Words with the Major Cards

Below is a list of the 22 Major Arcana cards with blank lines. Next to each card title, make a note of one or more key words or phrases that are most important to you when you're "reading a card." This exercise works best if you are in a state of mind that allows you to enjoy the moment. Have each major card available to view at the time you are considering its meanings. If it feels right, be willing to open your third eye and intuit the optimal message the images offer.

Example: The World—finding resolutions, freedom to express ideas

1 The Magician ....

....

2 The High Priestess ....

....

3 The Empress ....

....

4 The Emperor ....

....

5 The High Priest ....

....

6 The Lovers ....

....

7 The Chariot ....

....

8 Strength ....

....

9 The Hermit ....

....

10 The Wheel of Fortune ....

....

11 Justice ....

....

12 The Hanged Man ....

....

13 Death ....

....

14 Temperance ....

....

15 The Devil ....

....

16 The Tower ....

....

17 The Star ....

....

18 The Moon ....

....

19 The Sun ....

....

20 Judgment ....

....

21 The World ....

....

0 The Fool ....

....

The Wisdom Card Reading

After you have completed the above practice, take your major cards and, without looking at their images, shuffle them. Once you feel that your shuffle is complete, place them facedown on the table, with their backside facing you. Next, randomly draw a card for a one-card reading.

What card did you draw? Using the keywords and phrases that you wrote in the prior exercise, contemplate what this card is communicating to you in this moment. What wisdom or insight does it offer?

THE FOOL

Sometimes Foolishness Is Wisdom in Disguise

The Fool walks spontaneously in each moment, celebrating the beauty of life. Free from regrets, and from fears of not being good enough or of having stagnant worries about following the norm, he meanders mental and material mazes with acceptance, trust, and faith in whatever circumstance comes his way. Possessing a spiritual awareness, his generous nature and effortless way of being is comparable to a childlike innocence.

DIVINATORY MEANINGS

Central idea

Freedom

Key interpretations

Being free spirited, playful communications, independence, thinking outside the box, daring, feeling harmony with nature

Emotional associations

Love without fear, the trusting heart, unconditional acceptance, light hearted, soul-to-soul talks, contentment, fun loving

Dominant mood

Adventurous

Astrological link

Uranus

Planetary qualities

Originality, expect the unexpected, interacting with alchemical transformative energy, powerful and potent forces

Reversed card meaning

Acting foolish

UNDERSTANDING THE FOOL

Spirit Quest
Being Aware in the Present Moment

Keeping the spotlight of your attention focused in this very moment brings awareness. What do your body, mind, and emotions tell you in this very instant? What thoughts distract you from being in the here and now? If your attention is on the past, or your concerns are focused on the future, you'll be missing the gifts from the universe that only exist within the present. Noticing a fragrant rose sitting on your kitchen table, or a cat looking into your window, can become part of a picturesque diorama that inspires a soulful awareness of timelessness.

The present moment is a present to enjoy.

Tarot Notes

Tarot is said by many to be "The Fool's Journey." What does this mean to you? What is your strongest intuitive sense about The Fool?

....

....

....

....

....

....

....

If you plan to take your Tarot cards with you into the future, think about how you will assume your role as a reader. If someone calls you a fool, what can you tell yourself that reminds you to connect with your personal power?

....

....

....

....

....

....

....

What is the most foolish thing you have ever done? Imagine how The Fool would respond to your discussion of this experience. What advice might he give?

....

....

....

....

....

....

....

....

....

....

....

INTUITIVE PORTAL

Being in the "Now," an Inner-Dialogue Two-Card Reading

Like north on a compass, the true magic of the Tarot's Fool is always found within the "NOW" of the present moment. To help you connect with the voice of The Fool, take out The Fool card and place it on your table.

Now meditate to calm your mind, and shuffle your remaining Major Arcana cards. Without looking at the front of your cards, randomly select one card for insight into what the present offers. Next, turn this card face up and endeavor to interpret its symbols in relation to your present thoughts or questions. Now, imagine the central image on your selected card having a dialogue with The Fool. What do these two cards communicate to you? Does the conversation between the two card images give you any useful insights?

What insights can The Fool offer your randomly selected card?

PART THREE

ENDINGS INITIATE NEW BEGINNINGS

GOODBYE FOR NOW

Thank you 22 times infinity for the journaling that you've done in your playbook! Keep practicing to strengthen your relationship with your cards. Consistent practice will guide you on the path of personal experience toward learning to do divination. It might accelerate your success to sprinkle a little salt over your right shoulder for good luck, or maybe it won't. What's important is that you always carry a little extra love in your pocket, and when it feels right, sprinkle it like fairy dust to inspire an uplifting note to your readings.

You have arrived at the end of your playbook and are ready to begin a new Tarot chapter in your life. By writing down your ideas concerning the cards, you have gained clarity about their meaning and deepened your insight into your attitudes and perceptions about their images. By experiencing the Intuitive Portal and using the Skill-Building Practices, you have been working to solidify a foundation of knowledge that can support your intuitive practice. Like The Magician who is inspired to win and spins The Wheel of Fortune, proceed with trust in the skills that you are developing, and enjoy your journey.

Look through your third eye to intuit your Tarot path.

APPENDIX 1

Journal Template for Keeping Records of Readings

from *Tarot at a Crossroads*

My Journal

Today's Notes

Date and time of reading:

Name of person getting reading:

Age:

Divinatory or Representational Session:

What cards were drawn?

How were they placed on the table?

What topics were discussed?

Noteworthy information discovered during this experience:

My reaction:

APPENDIX 2

The Popular Three-Card Spread

from *Sacred Mysteries: The Chakra Oracle*

Meaning of the Card Positions in the Most Traditional of Three-Card Spreads

Card 1: Past

Card 2: Present

Card 3: Future

The Three-Card Spread offers a quick look into any type of situation and can be a gateway to understanding you or your client's emerging concerns. It can also act as a platform to build trust and confidence with the person you're reading.

After determining your or your client's question, shuffle and cut your deck into three stacks. Select three cards from the top of the middle stack and lay them in a straight horizontal line.

1. The first card on the left represents the past, or foundation, of the situation being questioned.
2. The second, or middle, card is associated with the present and concerns that are central to you or your client's outlook in the moment.
3. The third card, positioned to the right side of the other two cards, is viewed as the future, or the potential outcome of present concerns.

Once you've created a spread, reflect on the colors, the images, the meanings, and the titles of the cards. Look at each card individually and consider what each says as it stands alone. Then, look at the three as they are joined together, and think about how they speak to one another.

- ✦ What is their message?
- ✦ How do they make you feel?
- ✦ What moods and emotions do they trigger?
- ✦ What key images weave a story into a tapestry of constructive wisdom?
- ✦ What is the most important message communicated through your understanding of their meanings and their position in the layout?

APPENDIX 3

Pages For Journaling

....

....

....

....

....

....

....

....

....

....

....

....

....

....

....

....

....

....

....

....

....

BIBLIOGRAPHY

Amberstone, Ruth Ann, and Wald Amberstone. *Tarot Tips*. St. Paul, MN: Llewellyn, 2003.

Amberstone, Wald, and Ruth Ann Amberstone. *The Secret Language of Tarot*. San Francisco: Red Wheel / Weiser, 2008.

Crowley, Aleister. *The Book of Thoth*. York Beach, ME: Weiser Books, 2002.

Daniels, Kooch N., and Victor Daniels. *Tarot at a Crossroads: The Unexpected Meeting of Tarot & Psychology*. Atglen, PA: Schiffer, 2016.

Daniels, Kooch N., and Victor Daniels. *Tarot d'Amour: Find Love, Sex, and Romance in the Cards*. Boston and York Beach, ME: Red Wheel / Weiser, 2003.

Greer, Mary K. *Tarot Constellations: Patterns of Personal Destiny*. North Hollywood, CA: Newcastle, 1987.

Harish, Johari. *Numerology with Tantra, Ayurveda, and Astrology*. Rochester, VT: Destiny Books, 1990.

Kaplan, Stuart R. *Encyclopedia of Tarot, Vol. 1*. New York: US Games Systems, 1985.

Palladini, David, and Anastasia Haysler. *Painting the Soul: The Tarot Art of David Palladini*. San Francisco: Black Swan, 2013.

Place, Robert. *Alchemy and the Tarot*. Saugerties, NY: Hermes, 2011.

Pollack, Rachel. *Seventy-Eight Degrees of Wisdom: A Book of Tarot*. Rev. ed. San Francisco: Red Wheel / Weiser Books, 2007.

Wanless, James. *Voyager Tarot: Way of the Great Oracle*. Carmel, CA: Merrill-West, 1989.

ACKNOWLEDGMENTS

My deep appreciation goes to my daughters, Tara Daniels and Lila Welchel, for reading and commenting on my writing, and for their inspiration, giggles, and critiques. I give heartfelt thanks to Victor, my Ace of Cups, for his faith in me, and his untiring support for my mystical dreams, the encouragement to follow them, and sharing his wisdom with me. A silent shout-out goes to my family, especially Mikaila Beeler and Mark Murphy, who sent me graphics for this work. I can never thank my New Age community enough, and all the amazing Tarot people who have inspired my journey.

I'm so happy that my friends Jaen Martins and Jane Lasky gave my pages their Mercurial nods of approval. I especially want to thank Cris Wanzer, who edited my playbook, and my Schiffer editor, Dinah Roseberry, and her team, who graciously shaped my words into form on these pages. I especially want to thank Christopher R. McClure and Pete Schiffer, who accepted my manuscript and put it into Schiffer's RedFeather Mind, Body, Spirit queue. Also, I thank Steve Killey, who made my life easier by helping me create my art files.

I'm so appreciate and offer my heartfelt thanks to all the Tarot deck creators who kindly let me use their beautiful Major Arcana images from their magical decks. If I could play a soundtrack of loud applause for the hours, weeks, months, and years that it takes to create a deck, you would hear it now to honor Jude Simmons, Kristine Gorman, Robert Place, Anna Franklin, Marie White, Beth Seilonen, Anna Kahn and Russell Moon, Jasmine Beckett-Griffith and J. R. Rivera, Dinah Roseberry, Christine "Kesara" Dennett, Gina G. Thies, James Wanless, and Steven Bright, whose art you will see in these pages.

For all of you who trusted me to give you readings or take my classes, I feel so blessed for the opportunities to learn with you the mystical language of symbols. So many of you knowingly or unknowingly were my teachers, who helped me walk the cliff's edge while following The Fool's footprints. I can't thank enough those of you who have invited me to give talks at your events or conferences. I have been gifted with so much wisdom by discussing the Tarot at BATS, NWTS, Readers Studio, PantheoCon, and various academic conferences.

With great reverence, I give thanks to my unwavering, Truth-illuminating teachers: Vedic scholar and temple artist Sri Harish Johari, and Mata Amritanandamayi, the loving, hugging saint from southern India. Both embody the profound wisdom of The Hermit, who holds the star of heaven in his earthly lantern to shine light on the path to Higher awakening. Through the veil of time I can see them both giving me the thumbs up for not forgetting to say that I'm so grateful for the Cosmic Mother and her many invisible hues of grace and card intervention.

Lover of oracles, **Kooch N. Daniels, MA**, is a professional intuitive living in the San Francisco Bay area who has given many thousands of Tarot readings. Early in life, her interest in esoteric traditions motivated her to travel to India to study mysticism, and this experience was a turning point in using her intuitive abilities. Her fascination with what lies hidden behind the veil has inspired her study with Eastern mystical artist and philosopher Harish Johari, and the hugging saint from India, Sri Mata Amritanandamayi.

Kooch has been a keynote speaker for Readers Studio in New York City and has taught Tarot, divination, and intuitive arts at many venues both nationally and internationally. She is a host on the Psychic Talk Radio show *Kooch's Kosmic Café*.

With her husband, Victor, she has cowritten *Tarot at a Crossroads: The Unexpected Meeting of Tarot & Psychology*; *Tarot d'Amour: Find Love, Sex, and Romance in the Cards*; *Matrix Meditations for Developing the Mind-Heart Connection*; *Awakening the Chakras: The Seven Energy Centers in Your Daily Life*; and *Sacred Mysteries: The Chakra Oracle*. Also, she has written a book on palmistry, a Tarot novel, and a computerized program that divines online personal readings. You can contact her through her website: www.cybermystic.com.